OCEAN

PHOTOGRAPHED BY
**FRANK GREENAWAY
KIM TAYLOR & JANE BURTON**

WRITTEN BY
**THERESA GREENAWAY
CHRISTIANE GUNZI
& BARBARA TAYLOR**

DK

A DK PUBLISHING BOOK

Editors Alexandra Tinley, Deborah Murrell, Sue Copsey
Art editors Colin Walton, Floyd Sayers, Val Wright
Senior editor Christiane Gunzi
Illustrations Nick Hall, Nick Hewetson, Dan Wright
Production Louise Barratt
Index Jane Parker
U.S. Assistant editor Camela Decaire

Natural history consultants

Geoff Boxshall, Barry Clarke, Andy Currant, Theresa Greenaway,
Paul Hillyard, Gordon Howes, Judith Marshall, Tim Parmenter, Paul Pearce-Kelly,
Mark O'Shea, Matthew Robertson, Edward Wade, Karen Willson

Picture credits

Bruce Coleman Ltd Luiz Claudio Marigo 9tc, Charles and Sandra Hood 8c, Adrian Davies 10tr, Fred
Bruemmer 35tr / **Dave King** 10cr, 11tr, 35tl / **NHPA** David Woodfall 9tr , Kelvin Aitken 10tc / **Oxford
Scientific Films** Richard Packwood 9tl / **Planet Earth Pictures** / Peter David 11cl / **Colin Salmon** 8tr,
11tr / **Steve Shott** 11tc / **Richard Ward** 34cl / **Dan Wright** 34cl

First American Edition, 1994
10 9 8 7 6 5 4 3 2
Published in the United States by
DK Publishing, Inc., 95 Madison Avenue
New York, New York 10016

Compilation copyright © 1994 Dorling Kindersley Ltd., London
Text copyright © 1994, 1992
Illustration copyright © 1994, 1992

Part of the material included in this book originally appeared in
Look Closer: Coral Reef; Swamp Life; Tide Pool; and Shoreline.

CIP data is available.
ISBN 1-56458-775-4

Color reproduction by Colourscan, Singapore
Printed and bound in Italy by New Interlitho, Milan

Publisher's note
All measurements mentioned in the "Fact Files"
refer to the actual sizes of species photographed.

CONTENTS

Seas of the world 8

Wildlife of the ocean 10

Sea horse 12

Grape corals 13

Mandarin fish 14

Giant clam 16

Common octopuses 18

Emperor angelfish 20

Hermit crab 22

Lettuce slugs 24

Clown fish 26

Sea cucumbers 28

Strawberry shrimp 30

Tub gurnards 32

Wildlife of the shore 34

Queen scallops 36

Lesser weever fish 38

Seaweeds 40

Sea lemon 42

Oystercatcher 44

Dog whelk 46

Sea urchins 48

Starfish 50

Sea scorpion 52

Piecrust crabs 54

Sea anemones 56

King ragworms 58

Shannies and rocklings 60

Velvet crab 62

Sea peas and thrift 64

Natterjack toad 66

Fiddler crabs 68

Peacock worms 70

Mudskipper 72

Common lizards 74

Glossary 76

Index 77

SEAS OF THE WORLD

The sea is the largest habitat on Earth, covering two thirds of the planet. An ocean, such as the Pacific Ocean or the Atlantic Ocean, is simply a large expanse of sea. Within the ocean there are other habitats, including tropical coral reefs, vast underwater deserts, and huge deep sea trenches. In certain places the sea is deeper than the highest mountains. The sea divides naturally into two main habitats – the water itself and the seabed. Each of these habitats is home to a rich variety of wildlife.

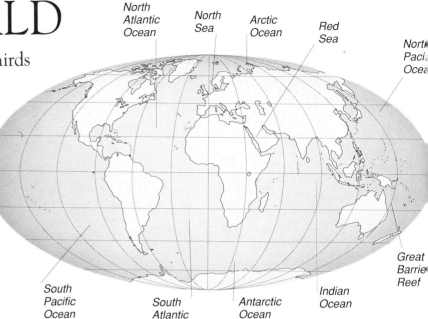

North Atlantic Ocean
North Sea
Arctic Ocean
Red Sea
Nort Paci Ocea
South Pacific Ocean
South Atlantic Ocean
Antarctic Ocean
Indian Ocean
Great Barrie Reef

CORAL REEFS

In shallow waters around tropical islands, where the temperature is above 66°F, coral reefs grow. Coral reefs consist of the limestone shells made by tiny animals called coral polyps, which look like sea anemones. Many colorful tropical fish live in the warm waters of coral reefs. Some fish that live among the corals have slim bodies to allow them to slip into cracks and crevices. Others have hard mouths so that they can feed on the coral.

SEASHOR

The area where the sea meets the land known as the seashore. Every piece of la has a seashore, and no two stretches of sho are the same. Seashores are shaped by power of the wind and waves, and constantly changing as the sea moves sa and pebbles up and down the beach. kinds of wildlife have made their homes a adapted to life in this salty environme

Emperor angelfish

Sea horse

Common octopus

Lesser weever fish

CONSERVATION

In many countries, people are trying to protect the nesting sites of birds, reptiles, and other animals. On the Greek island of Zakynthos, the nesting season for loggerhead turtles is midsummer, when thousands of tourists visit on vacation. The Greek government has limited access to the beaches at certain times so that the turtles can breed in safety.

THREATS TO SEA LIFE

The wildlife of seas and seashores is threatened in various ways; by litter, industrial waste, sewage dumping, overfishing, and by oil spills. When oil leaks out of a ship at sea, it forms an oil slick on the water, which is washed onto the seashore. Oil kills all kinds of plants, fish, birds, and mammals, and it spoils beaches, too.

CONTINENTAL SHELVES

Around most of the large land masses that we call continents, the seafloor slopes gently. These shallow sloping areas are called continental shelves, and they can be up to 219 yards deep. These waters are rich in sea life because they receive nutrients washed off the land and into the sea by rivers. Sunlight reaches down through about 110 yards of water, so plants are able to grow here as well.

TIDES

Twice every day the sea rises and falls with the tides. This is caused by the gravitational pull of the moon and the sun. As the moon moves around the earth, it pulls on the oceans. When the sun, earth, and moon are in line, and the moon is new or full, the pull is very powerful, causing the water to leap high up the shore. This is called a spring tide. When the moon is half full, there are neap tides, which reach only a short way up the shore.

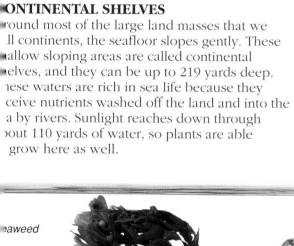

Velvet crab

Periwinkle

Seaweed

Sea lemon

WILDLIFE OF THE OCEAN

Life began in the water about 3,000 million years ago, and the seas still support the greatest range of wildlife of any habitat, including hundreds of different fish. Animals and plants have adapted to living at different levels. Close to the surface, where the water is warm, there are many kinds of fish. As the water gets deeper, it gets colder and darker, until there is no light, and possibly no life at all.

OCEAN MAMMALS

Ocean-dwelling mammals include dolphins, porpoises, and whales. These creatures have developed a streamlined shape to help them move swiftly through water. They also have a thick layer of fat beneath their skin to keep them warm.

BIRDS

Many seabirds are expert divers, able to plunge into the water from a great heigh to catch fish. Birds such as gannets often stay at sea for months at a time and only return to the shore to breed. Their large, powerful wings enable them to glide and hover on the wind without having to lan

SEA ANEMONES

Although they may look like plants, sea anemones are really carnivorous animals. They live attached to rocks or buried in the sand on the seashore and in shallow waters. Sea anemones have poisonous tentacles to paralyze their victims, some tropical species are powerful enough to harm a human.

Sea anemone

Clown fish

Thick-lipped gray mullet

Scorpion fish

FISH

Each species of fish is adapted to its particular environment, whether it lives on the seabed, among coral, or in the open ocean. Some fish are peaceful herbivores that live together in huge shoals, feeding on weeds. Others are predators that prey on smaller fish. All fish breathe underwater using gills, and they swim and steer in the water using fins.

MOLLU

There are about 51,000 speci mollusks. They make up the sec largest group of animals in the w All mollusks have soft bodies, and have a hard, protective s

Sea cucumber

Giant clam

FOOD CHAINS AND WEBS

In every kind of habitat, including the sea, there are food chains. In a simple food chain, a plant is eaten by an herbivore, which in turn is eaten by a carnivore. But many animals have more than one source of food, so the different food chains join up to form a food web. Food webs are often very complicated. This picture shows a simple ocean food web.

Plants are always at the bottom of a food chain. In this food web, microscopic plants, called phytoplankton, are eaten by microscopic animals, called zooplankton, and by common mussels, too.

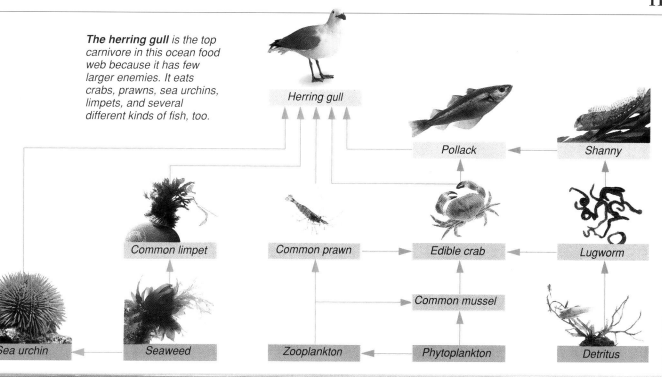

The herring gull is the top carnivore in this ocean food web because it has few larger enemies. It eats crabs, prawns, sea urchins, limpets, and several different kinds of fish, too.

Herring gull

Pollack — Shanny

Common limpet — Common prawn — Edible crab ← Lugworm

Sea urchin — Seaweed — Zooplankton — Common mussel — Phytoplankton — Detritus

DEEP-SEA LIFE

The deepest parts of the ocean are cold and dark, and scientists have discovered very little about this mysterious habitat. A surprising amount of creatures have adapted to life in the dark, including this

strange-looking deep-sea anglerfish. It swims along with its huge mouth gaping wide to help catch food, because it cannot see in the dark. There is a special light on its head to attract unsuspecting prey.

PLANTS

Most sea plants are found in the shallow waters of continental shelves. These plants consist of red, brown and green seaweeds, including wracks and kelps. Minute plants, known as phytoplankton, live in the surface waters of oceans all over the world.

CORALS

Coral reefs are home to a rich variety of wildlife. Corals themselves can only survive in clean, warm, salty water at shallow enough levels for sunlight to reach them.

Grape coral

Red seaweed

SEA HORSE

IT IS HARD TO BELIEVE that the sea horse is a fish. It has a head like a horse, a pouch like a kangaroo, and a tail for holding on to things, like a monkey. A sea horse can change color to match its habitat and hide from enemies. This is useful because it cannot swim fast to escape danger. These shy, peaceful creatures spend most of the day among coral waiting for food, such as shrimps, to pass within reach. During courtship, sea horses dance with their tails twined together. The female lays her eggs in a pouch on the front of the male's body. The eggs develop inside the pouch and the young emerge after two to seven weeks. As soon as they are born, young sea horses must fend for themselves.

DROPPING ANCHOR

The sea horse uses its strong, supple tail to anchor itself firmly to corals, seaweed, and sponges. This prevents the sea horse from being thrown around and injured by waves or underwater currents.

The fin on the back beats as many as 20 to 35 times a second.

These small fins look like ears. The sea horse flaps them to steer itself through the water.

To rise up, the sea horse straightens its tail. It curls its tail to sink down.

The sea horse's eyes move independently, so it can look in two directions at once.

This transparent fin sweeps back and forth to slowly push the sea horse through the water.

Close up, you can see ridges where the bony plates inside the body join to form the skeleton.

Its jaws are long and hollow, like a drinking straw.

FACT FILE
Name Sea horse
Hippocampus kuda
Size 4.5 in long
Distribution Southeast Asia

NOISY EATER

The sea horse has no teeth and swallows its food whole. It sucks up shrimps with its long, hollow jaws, making a clicking noise that can be heard some distance away. Sea horses feed almost all day long. They eat enormous amounts because they have no stomach in which to store food.

GRAPE CORALS

THESE BEAUTIFUL GRAPE corals may look like unusual plants, but they are really carnivorous (meat-eating) animals. Corals are related to jellyfish and sea anemones. Like them, they use stinging cells to defend themselves and catch their food. A coral colony (group) like this one is made up of hundreds of individual creatures, called polyps. The polyps divide into two over and over again to form exact copies of themselves. They also produce eggs that, when fertilized, develop into larvae. The larvae swim around in the sea until they reach a suitable spot to settle down and develop into adults. Over thousands of years, the skeletons of dead corals build up on top of each other to form a reef.

When this coral polyp is open, you can see its many smooth tentacles.

DEADLY HARPOONS
Corals cannot move, so they rely on the movement of the water to bring their food to them. Their poisonous tentacles paralyze prey, then pass it to the mouth. Each tentacle of this grape coral is about the size of your finger. It feeds at night, on microscopic animals.

FACT FILE
Name Grape coral
Plerogyra sinuosa
Size Tentacle 2.5 in long
Distribution Australia

MANDARIN FISH

THE BRILLIANTLY COLORED mandarin fish lives near the bottom of the sea. It spends most of its time hidden in crevices or cracks in coral reefs. The mandarin fish feeds on smaller fish and other creatures that swim or float past it in the water. It also nibbles at millions of tiny plants, called algae, that grow on the coral reefs. The bold patterns on its skin help protect the fish from enemies by warning them of the bad-tasting mucus that its body produces. The mandarin fish can also deter larger fish from attacking it by raising the long spine on its back. This trick makes the fish appear larger than it really is.

There are no eyelids or tear ducts on the eyes. The seawater cleans the eyes instead.

The small, downturned mouth is a good shape for nibbling food from coral reefs.

Bony covers protect the gills, which take in oxygen from the water.

This long, pointed spine is the first ray of the front fin on the fish's back. These back fins are called dorsal fins.

Both eyes stick out so the fish can see in front and to the sides. Mandarin fish can see things in color.

The tail fin moves from side to side to push and steer the fish through the water.

This ventral fin, together with the dorsal fins, helps the fish stay upright in the water.

SIXTH SENSE

Like all fish, the mandarin fish has a line of pores, or holes, connected to a tubular canal under the scales. This canal is called the lateral line. It runs along each side of the fish's body and detects movements and pressure changes in the water. These help the fish to find its way around and to sense danger – or a possible meal.

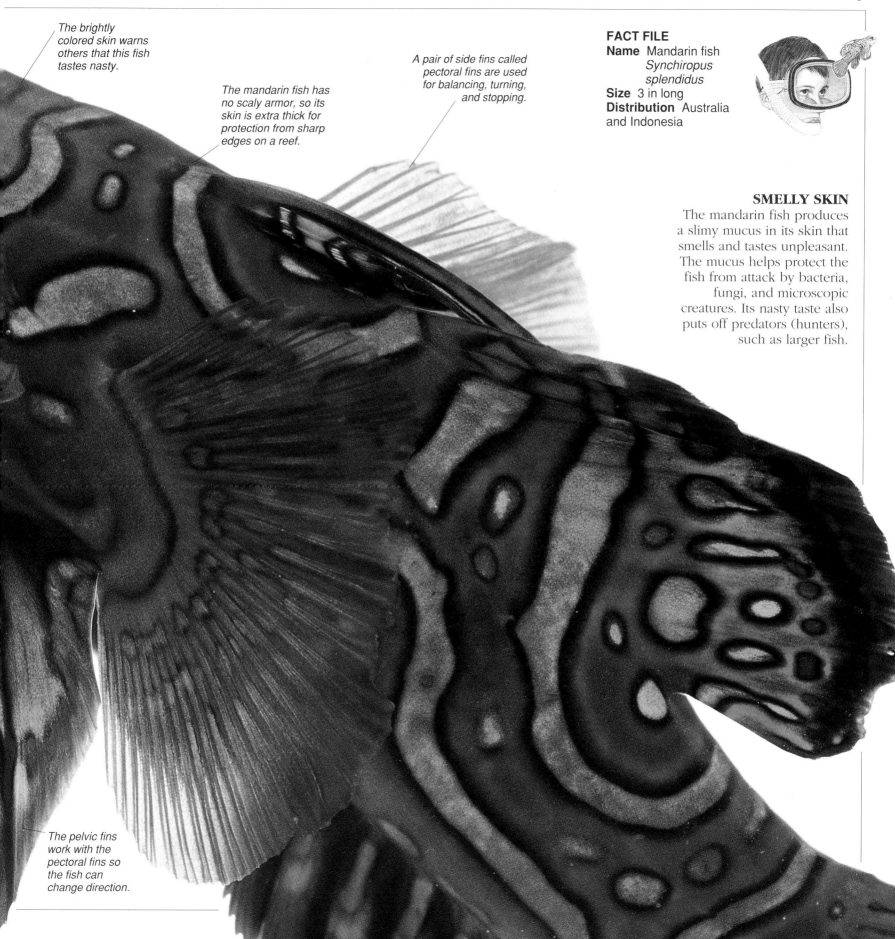

The brightly colored skin warns others that this fish tastes nasty.

The mandarin fish has no scaly armor, so its skin is extra thick for protection from sharp edges on a reef.

A pair of side fins called pectoral fins are used for balancing, turning, and stopping.

FACT FILE
Name Mandarin fish *Synchiropus splendidus*
Size 3 in long
Distribution Australia and Indonesia

SMELLY SKIN
The mandarin fish produces a slimy mucus in its skin that smells and tastes unpleasant. The mucus helps protect the fish from attack by bacteria, fungi, and microscopic creatures. Its nasty taste also puts off predators (hunters), such as larger fish.

The pelvic fins work with the pectoral fins so the fish can change direction.

GIANT CLAM

THIS COLORFUL giant clam is a soft-bodied animal that lives inside a strong, hard shell. The shell is made of two halves that can open and close. A clam opens its shell to feed and shuts it tight when threatened. Algae grows on the clam's body, absorbing some of its waste products, and in return, the clam feeds on some of the algae. It also eats microscopic plants, called plankton, that drift past in the seawater. Clams develop from tiny eggs that hatch into larvae. The larvae swim around for about nine days, then settle down on a reef to grow into adults. Giant clams do not move once they are mature, and they sometimes grow as large as three feet across.

SUPER SIPHON

Clams have no head, so they cannot breathe and feed the same way other animals do. Instead, they have two openings called siphons. The small siphon allows water full of oxygen and food to pass into the body. The large siphon squirts waste products out of the body.

Waste products leave the body through this large siphon.

The two sides of the mantle join together so that the clam's body is completely enclosed and cannot be seen by predators.

Ridges and grooves on the shell make it strong. They also help disguise the clam when it closes its shell.

LIVING LARDER

The green patches on the clam are colonies of algae. Algae lives in the part called the mantle, the frilly layer between the clam's soft body and its hard shell. The algae grows and multiplies throughout the clam's life, so the clam always has a good source of food.

FACT FILE
Name Giant clam
      Tridacna species
Size 6 in across
Distribution Australia

HINGED HOME

The clam first makes its shell from chemicals in the water, then the mantle gradually adds layers of chalk to the shell to make it grow bigger. The shell supports and protects the clam's soft body. The matching halves are joined together with a hinge, and strong muscles close them together for protection. The body of the clam is joined to the shell by muscles.

Simple eyes are all the clam needs.

Algae grows in the large, fleshy mantle. It produces its own food by using the energy in sunlight.

EYES EVERYWHERE
Rows of sensitive eyes along the edge of the mantle can detect changes in light and shadow. This helps the clam to see predators in time to heave its shell slowly shut.

There is a small siphon that sucks in water.

COMMON OCTOPUSES

FACT FILE
Name Common octopus
Octopus vulgaris
Size 9.5 in long,
including tentacles
Distribution Worldwide

OCTOPUSES ARE CLEVER animals that can learn and remember things. They are shy and spend most of their time shuffling around on coral reefs or hiding inside their homes, which they build from piles of stones. This common octopus sometimes lurks inside coral caves and attacks crabs and shellfish as they pass by. Octopuses are related to mollusks, such as clams, but they do not have a shell and they can swim much faster than most shellfish. A female octopus lays long strings of eggs and hangs them from the roof of her home. She keeps the eggs clean and guards them so carefully that she does not have time to eat. After about six weeks, the eggs hatch into tiny octopuses. Soon afterward, the female octopus dies of starvation.

Scientists believe this blue spot may be an identifying mark that enables one octopus to recognize another of its kind.

The arms feel and taste things. They are also used for walking and holding food.

Strong suckers down each arm help the octopus hold on to rocks and food.

ARMS EVERYWHERE

An octopus has eight writhing arms with strong suckers that curl around victims to prevent them from escaping. The octopus bites its prey with a horny beak and injects it with poison and special juices to make it easier to digest. Then the octopus uses its filelike tongue, called a radula, to tear off pieces of flesh.

The funnel helps propel the octopus through the water.

THE JET SET

The octopus swims by jet propulsion. As it squeezes a jet of water out through its funnel, its body is pushed forward through the water. The hot gases rushing out of the back of a jet engine push an airplane forward in a similar way. The octopus steers itself through the water by directing the jet stream.

Each sucker has millions of microscopic hairs for feeling surfaces.

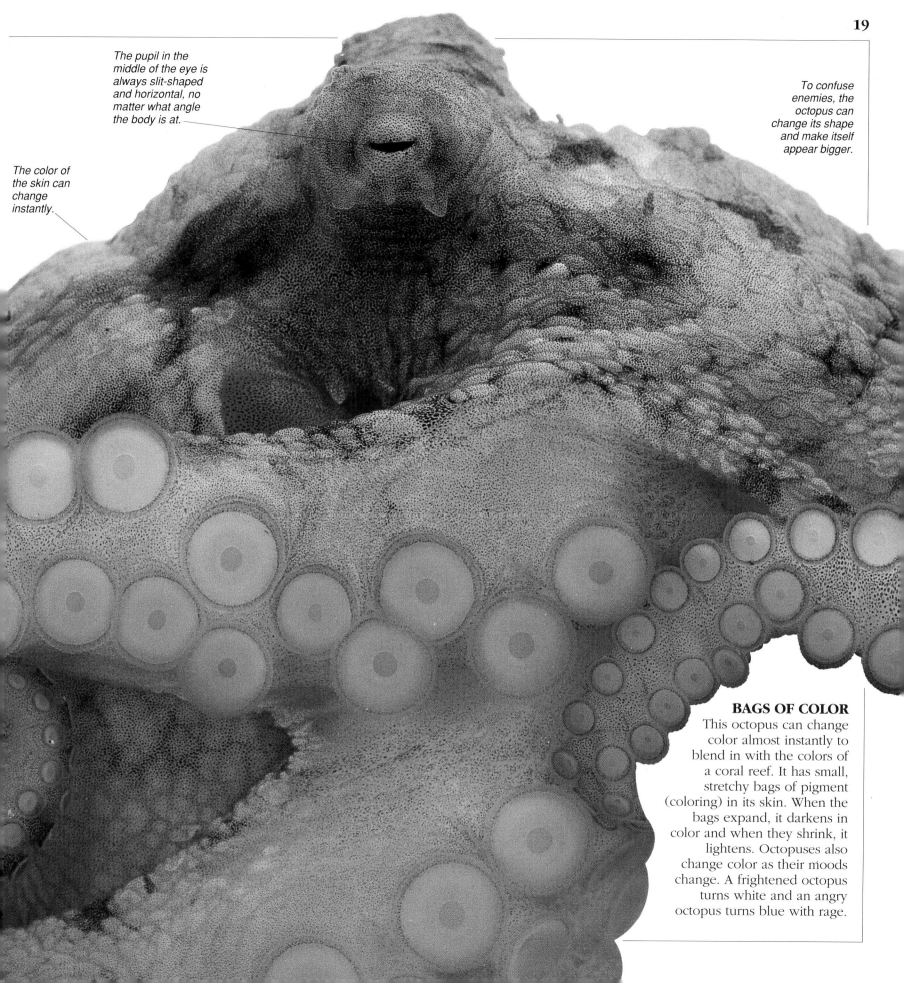

The pupil in the middle of the eye is always slit-shaped and horizontal, no matter what angle the body is at.

To confuse enemies, the octopus can change its shape and make itself appear bigger.

The color of the skin can change instantly.

BAGS OF COLOR

This octopus can change color almost instantly to blend in with the colors of a coral reef. It has small, stretchy bags of pigment (coloring) in its skin. When the bags expand, it darkens in color and when they shrink, it lightens. Octopuses also change color as their moods change. A frightened octopus turns white and an angry octopus turns blue with rage.

EMPEROR ANGELFISH

THE BEAUTIFUL EMPEROR angelfish hovers in the water near small caves in a coral reef so that it can shoot inside if it senses danger. Its flat body allows it to slip easily through narrow gaps in the coral. This agile fish spends most of the day nibbling at sponges on a reef. Once two angelfish have mated, they remain together for the rest of their lives. The pair live in their own territory, a small patch of reef that they defend against other angelfish. The female lays eggs that are fertilized by the male. The eggs float in the sea, away from the reef and the many enemies that might eat them. Larvae hatch out of the eggs, and eventually they change into little fish and find a new coral reef.

COLORFUL SIGNALS

The vibrant colors and patterns of this adult emperor angelfish help it recognize others of its own kind. Colors can also attract a mate and may become brighter in the breeding season. Angelfish usually live in water that is at least 48 feet deep. Their bright colors show up well in the dim light.

There is one eye on each side of the head for good all-around vision.

The strong teeth inside the mouth pull pieces of sponge, coral, and algae from a reef.

The winglike pectoral fins balance and turn the fish.

The tail fin is called the caudal fin. It pushes the fish along and helps it steer.

SCHOOL UNIFORM

Young emperor angelfish have blue bodies with white circles. They often swim in groups, called schools. Their uniform appearance helps protect them from attack by the adults. The colors of the young fish are very different from those of the adults, and they change gradually as the fish mature.

FACT FILE
Name Emperor angelfish
Pomacanthus imperator
Size 4.5 in long (adult)
Distribution Asia, Australia, and the Red Sea

These light-colored rings attract predators to the fish's tail rather than its head. If the attacker falls for the decoy, the angelfish's head is safe.

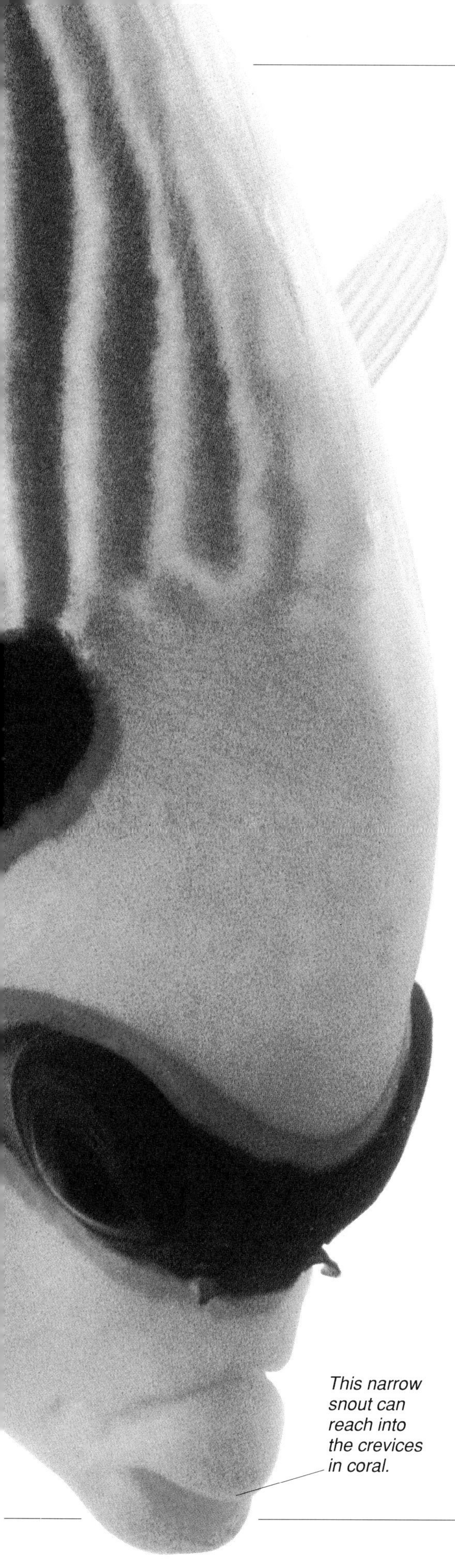

Close up, you can see the overlapping scales that protect the body.

This narrow snout can reach into the crevices in coral.

The dark blue color and light pattern help disguise the young fish from enemies.

HERMIT CRAB

THIS EXTRAORDINARY CRAB spends its life inside another animal's shell. Hermit crabs like this one protect the soft rear part of their body, called the abdomen, by living in the empty shells of whelks and other sea snails. The coiled abdomen fits inside the shell, and a hook on the end helps the crab keep a firm grip on it. The crab can stretch its legs out of the shell to pull itself along. The hermit crab takes its home with it wherever it goes. When the crab grows too big for one shell, it simply moves to a larger one. Female hermit crabs lay eggs, which they carry around on one side of the abdomen. The eggs hatch into tiny larvae that drift in the sea with the plankton. Eventually the larvae settle down to become adults and find a shell-home of their own.

Bright dots on the body help disguise the crab on a coral reef.

The crab's legs are hairy. These hairs, called setae, are very sensitive. They help the crab to feel its way around. They also detect the movements of food and predators.

At the first sign of danger, the crab quickly pulls its whole body back inside this conch shell for protection.

NEW CLOTHES FOR OLD

The hard outer skin, called the exoskeleton, is on the front part of the body. It does not expand as the crab grows. Instead, the crab molts its exoskeleton from time to time. A soft new exoskeleton grows beneath the old one, which splits so that the crab can pull itself out. The new exoskeleton takes time to harden.

FACT FILE
Name Hermit crab
Dardanus megistos
Size 3 in long, including shell
Distribution Australia, eastern Africa, the Hawaiian Islands, the Red Sea, and Southeast Asia

HOUSE HUNTING

Hermit crabs must search for an empty shell that is the right size. Before moving in, they investigate and explore the shell with their claws to see if it is large enough. Some hermit crabs live inside tubes in coral or wood instead of shells.

Large eyes peer out from the ends of long stalks.

The antennae (feelers) are sensitive to touch.

Feathery mouthparts are used for feeding.

MUD, GLORIOUS MUD

The hermit crab uses its mouthparts to sift through sand or mud for food particles. It also scavenges for dead animals or plants, and sometimes it even catches small fish.

CLEVER CLAWS

Hermit crabs have ten legs. The front two legs are a pair of large pincers or nippers, used for feeding, cleaning, and defense. When a hermit crab senses danger, it quickly draws back inside its shell and seals the entrance with its hard claws.

The exoskeleton is very hard, so the legs are jointed. This allows them to bend.

The claws are used for fighting, catching food, and barricading the crab's shell from attackers.

LETTUCE SLUGS

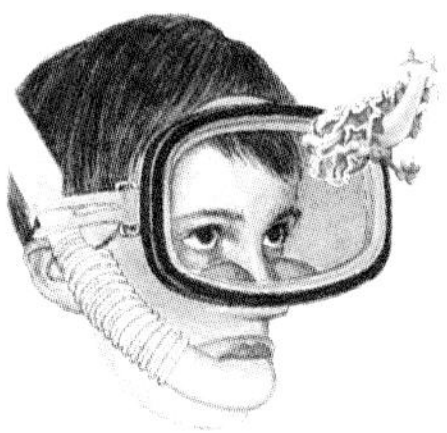

SLUGS ARE RELATED TO garden snails, but they have no shell to protect their soft bodies. Most sea slugs have very special diets. Some eat only a few types of sponge, while others feed on coral or even other sea slugs. This lettuce slug feeds on algae. Like snails, sea slugs scrape up food with their strong jaws and radula. Sometimes they mix the food with slimy mucus and suck it up instead. Each sea slug is both male and female at the same time. This makes it easier for them to find a mate and it means that every sea slug can lay eggs. The eggs hatch into larvae that swim around for a while until they find a good place to settle down and grow into adults.

FACT FILE
Name Lettuce slug
Elysia crispata
Size 1 in long
Distribution The Caribbean and Florida

This frilly edge on the body takes in oxygen and absorbs sunlight.

The bright green color indicates that this slug eats algae.

The soft body has no shell for protection.

A sea slug crawls over the slippery seaweed on its flat, slimy foot.

TERRIBLE TASTE
Lettuce slugs may look like a tasty salad, but they have special glands in their skin that produce a bad-tasting substance. This discourages predators from eating them.

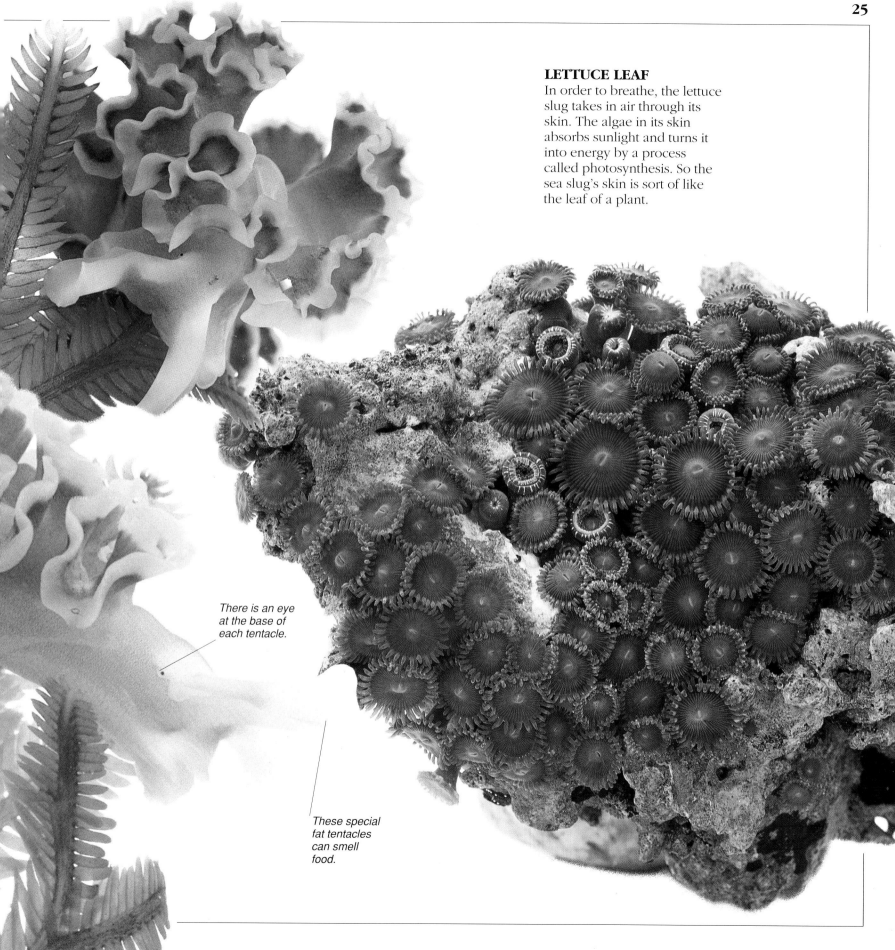

LETTUCE LEAF
In order to breathe, the lettuce slug takes in air through its skin. The algae in its skin absorbs sunlight and turns it into energy by a process called photosynthesis. So the sea slug's skin is sort of like the leaf of a plant.

There is an eye at the base of each tentacle.

These special fat tentacles can smell food.

CLOWN FISH

THE CLOWN FISH LIVES on a coral reef in
harmony with another creature, the sea anemone
(see p.56). Sea anemones have poisonous tentacles
for stinging prey, and a clown fish darts into an
anemone's tentacles for safety at the first sign of
danger. In return for the protection of the tentacles,
the fish frightens enemies away from the anemone.
The clown fish also lays its eggs and rears its young
among its friend's tentacles. Both creatures are
protected from the poison themselves by a layer of
slimy mucus covering their skin. Clown fish have
never been seen living without sea anemones,
but sea anemones can survive on their own.

(see p.56)

FACT FILE
Name Clown fish
Amphiprion species
Size 6.5 in long
Distribution Australia

Tentacles grasp
prey and push it
toward the
mouth opening.

CLOWN COSTUME

The clown fish's bright colors mean that it cannot
easily hide from its enemies. But it can escape by
swimming among the tentacles of the anemone,
which makes it hard to catch. The colors and
patterns of the fish may also warn predators of
the anemone's poisonous tentacles, and help
keep both animals safe.

Hundreds of
stinging tentacles
catch food.

The large
eyes watch
for danger.

The clown fish's
mouth has a hard
jaw for nibbling at
algae on coral
reefs. It also feeds
on tiny creatures
called plankton.

The base of the
anemone's body is
attached to a rock
for support.

Side fins are used
for steering and
changing direction.

SEA CUCUMBERS

SAUSAGE-SHAPED SEA CUCUMBERS crawl over coral reefs on their tube feet, picking up particles of food with their sticky tentacles. These extraordinary animals are related to starfish and sea urchins and have lived on Earth for millions of years. The sea cucumber has no head, just a mouth at one end and an opening for waste removal at the other end. Their bodies are bendable and can easily change color and shape. Some sea cucumbers can produce poisonous, sticky threads to trap enemies. Sea cucumbers lay eggs that develop into larvae. The larvae are small and transparent and drift along in the sea, eventually settling down to grow into adults. Adult sea cucumbers lay thousands of eggs because many of the larvae are eaten and only a few survive to become adults.

FEATHERY FEELERS
Around the mouth, there are many large, feathery tentacles. They are covered with mucus. The tentacles feel for tiny plants and animals on a coral reef. The sea cucumber sucks the food off the tentacles with its fleshy lips.

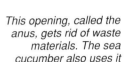

FACT FILE
Name Sea cucumber
Paracucumaria tricolor
Size 7 in long
Distribution Australia

This opening, called the anus, gets rid of waste materials. The sea cucumber also uses it when it is breathing.

The feathery shape of the tentacles helps them catch as much food as possible.

Particles of food catch on the sticky mucus that covers each tentacle.

Sea cucumbers can pull these tentacles back inside the body to protect them.

The mouth is in the middle of the tentacles.

Suckers on the ends of the tube feet grip onto rocks as the sea cucumber walks.

The tough, spiny skin discourages enemies from eating the sea cucumber.

WALKING ON THE WATER

Many sea cucumbers have rows of brightly colored tube feet along the sides of their bodies. Water fills the tube feet so that they become stiff and work like levers to push the sea cucumber along over rocks. Suckers on the ends of the feet grip onto rocks and other slippery surfaces.

Each tube foot is full of water.

STRAWBERRY SHRIMP

THIS STRAWBERRY SHRIMP is one of many kinds of tiny, brightly colored shrimps that live on a coral reef. Strawberry shrimps are very shy and hide in natural crevices in the coral or dig burrows in the sand. Strong exoskeletons help protect their soft bodies. Shrimps have paddlelike back legs, called swimmerets, on the abdomen, which help them to swim fast. Female strawberry shrimps carry their eggs on the swimmerets. A sticky cement holds the eggs in place while they develop. After a few weeks, the eggs hatch into larvae and swim away from their mother. Eventually, the larvae change into tiny versions of the adults and settle down on a reef to make homes of their own.

The shrimp uses its walking legs to preen (clean) its antennae.

BALANCING ACT
At the base of the antennae is a special organ called a statocyst, which helps the shrimp to balance. This organ is like a sack containing sand or grit. Each time the shrimp moves, the grit moves inside the sack. Cells in the sack send information to the brain, so the shrimp can determine its position in the water.

There is a special organ inside here for balancing.

Each antenna is made up of lots of segments so it can bend.

CLEANING SERVICE
The shrimp strains particles of food from the water with its fringed mouthparts. Strawberry shrimps are known as cleaners because they use their mouthparts to remove parasites from the scales of fish. They also scavenge for dead animal or plant remains and catch living prey, such as plankton.

The two pairs of antennae detect chemicals in the water and help the shrimp find food.

If the shrimp loses one of its claws, a new one grows to replace it.

The shrimp uses its claws, called chelipeds, to grasp or pick up food and also to dig in the sand.

FACT FILE
Name Strawberry shrimp
Lysmata debelius
Size 1.25 in long
Distribution Southeast Asia

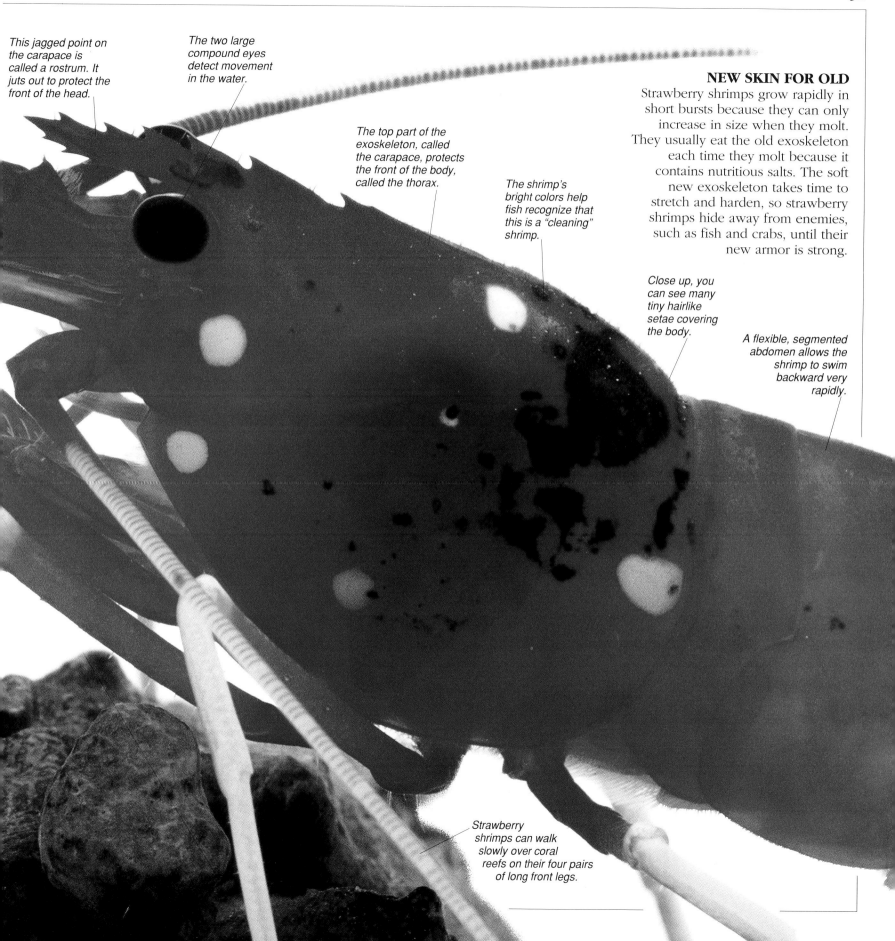

This jagged point on the carapace is called a rostrum. It juts out to protect the front of the head.

The two large compound eyes detect movement in the water.

The top part of the exoskeleton, called the carapace, protects the front of the body, called the thorax.

The shrimp's bright colors help fish recognize that this is a "cleaning" shrimp.

NEW SKIN FOR OLD
Strawberry shrimps grow rapidly in short bursts because they can only increase in size when they molt. They usually eat the old exoskeleton each time they molt because it contains nutritious salts. The soft new exoskeleton takes time to stretch and harden, so strawberry shrimps hide away from enemies, such as fish and crabs, until their new armor is strong.

Close up, you can see many tiny hairlike setae covering the body.

A flexible, segmented abdomen allows the shrimp to swim backward very rapidly.

Strawberry shrimps can walk slowly over coral reefs on their four pairs of long front legs.

TUB GURNARDS

WALKING SLOWLY OVER the ocean floor, tub gurnards use their fingerlike rays at the front of their pectoral fins to push themselves along. These fish usually live in schools, in shallow water near the shore. There they search for food in the sand, mud, and pebbles. Tub gurnards eat many kinds of small fish, as well as shrimps, crabs, and sea-dwelling worms. In summer, each female gurnard lays thousands of tiny eggs that measure less than a millimeter across. At first, the young that hatch out of the eggs float in the water close to the surface. But there they are easy prey for larger fish. So when the surviving young are fully developed, they swim down into the ocean to begin their adult lives.

FACT FILE
Name Tub gurnard
Trigla lucerna
Size 1 ft long
Distribution Europe

COLOR CHANGE
This young tub gurnard's pectoral fins have bright blue edges and greenish-blue spots at the base. As the fish grows larger, these striking colors will change. A fully grown tub gurnard has brilliant red and blue pectoral fins with green edges.

The fish uses these large pectoral fins for balancing and turning.

The pointed snout is a good shape for scooping up food from the seabed.

The dorsal fin stands up to keep the fish steady in the water.

Mottled brown colors help the fish blend in with the sand and shingle of the seabed.

The tail fin pushes the fish through the water.

There are no scales on the head. Instead, it is protected by small, bony plates and spines.

FEELING FINS

The three rays at the front of each pectoral fin work like feelers. The tub gurnard uses them for walking, and for poking around for food on the seabed. They are separate from the rest of the rays on the fin, which are joined together by a thin skin, called a membrane. Each of the front rays can move on its own, the same way your fingers do.

Like all fish, the gurnard breathes through gills. These are under the bony gill covers on each side of its head.

The lateral line runs down each side of the body, detecting movement in the water.

Fishes' eyes do not have eyelids. Instead, seawater keeps them moist and clean.

If danger threatens, the pectoral fins flick sand and gravel over the body to hide it from enemies.

WILDLIFE OF THE SHORE

LIFE ON THE SHORE is different from life in the sea because of the tides. Seashore wildlife has to survive both wet and dry conditions. Some animals are covered by water for part of the day, then exposed to the sun and wind for many hours. On a rocky shore there are pebbles to cling to, and cracks to shelter in when the tide goes out. But a sandy shore offers nowhere to hide, so animals living there must burrow in the sand or swim in and out with the tide.

SEASHORE PLANTS

Plants on a seashore are exposed to wind and salt blowing in from the sea. Not many flowering plants are able to survive these salty conditions. Tough, hardy plants, such as marram grass and sand reed, survive due to their long dense roots. These roots also protect the sand dunes. They hold sand in place that would otherwise be badly trampled or blown away by the wind. These plants are protected by law in some areas.

ZONES OF THE SHORELINE

The shore is divided into different zones by the tides, and each zone has its own particular wildlife. The lowest part of the shore is only exposed to the air when the tide is at its lowest. The upper, middle, and lower zones are exposed twice a day when the tide goes out. The sea only reaches the splash zone, at the highest part of the shore, during stormy weather or when there are spring tides, which leap up the beach. This picture shows you which animals and plants can be found in the different zones of the shore. It also shows you where the low and high tide marks are.

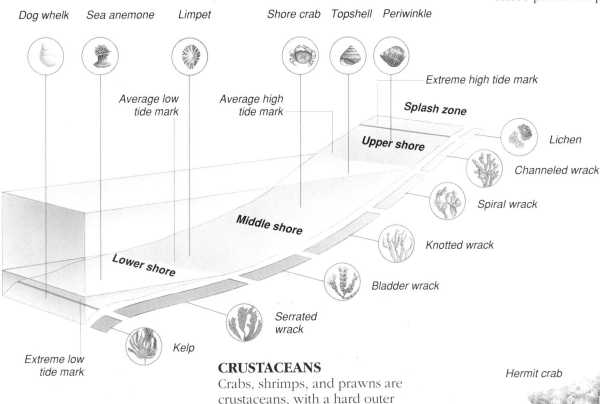

Dog whelk · Sea anemone · Limpet · Shore crab · Topshell · Periwinkle

Average low tide mark
Average high tide mark
Extreme high tide mark
Splash zone
Upper shore
Lichen
Channeled wrack
Spiral wrack
Middle shore
Knotted wrack
Lower shore
Bladder wrack
Serrated wrack
Extreme low tide mark
Kelp

CRUSTACEANS

Crabs, shrimps, and prawns are crustaceans, with a hard outer casing to their bodies. Other shelled animals called mollusks also live on the shore, including scallops, mussels, and whelks.

Hermit crab

Queen scallops

ESTUARIES
An estuary is where a river meets the sea. As a river flows into the sea it carries silt along and deposits it as mud banks. These banks form rich feeding grounds for wading birds. Animals living in estuaries are among the most adaptable of all sea creatures because they can put up with the constant change in salt levels in the water and the problems of living in mud.

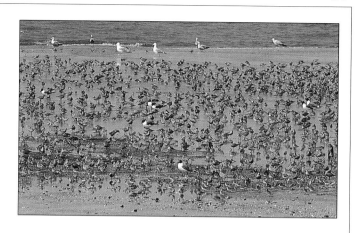

REPTILES
Lizards, snakes, and turtles belong to a large class of animals called reptiles. Some reptiles, such as saltwater crocodiles and loggerhead turtles swim well and live in water. Others live on the shore, such as this common lizard.

Common lizard

AMPHIBIANS
Animals that can live on land and in water are called amphibians. Amphibians only live in fresh water, which they need to keep their skin moist for respiration. Some species hibernate in the sand dunes of the seashore during the cold months, then, in the spring, they migrate to fresh water to breed.

DE POOLS
e main problem for most seashore imals and plants is how to avoid ying out between the tides. But in a e pool there are different problems the wildlife. The levels of oxygen d salt in the water are constantly anging, and the temperature is, too. t many species are able to survive ch changes. Some animals take elter under cool rocks and moist weed so their bodies do not dry t before the tide comes in again.

SEABIRDS
Many birds depend on the rich supply of food in the sea and along the shoreline. Some scavenge for insects, mollusks, and crustaceans on the beach, while others find their food by diving for fish under the water.

ift

Oystercatcher

Natterjack toad

QUEEN SCALLOPS

QUEEN SCALLOPS LIE on the muddy seabed close to the shore in colonies, feeding on tiny algae. Scallops are called bivalves because their shells have two halves, called valves. The valves are strong and hard, and protect the soft body inside. Scallops are much better swimmers than other shelled sea creatures, such as mussels. They flap along through the water in a series of jerks. In summer, scallops release clouds of eggs into the water. A tiny larva hatches out of each egg and swims around for about three weeks. Then it anchors itself to a surface, such as a piece of seaweed, with strong threads that it produces inside its body. About a year later, when the shell is fully developed, the scallop swims off to join a colony of adults.

WATER JETS

Scallops swim by opening and shutting the two halves of their shell, much like clapping. This forces water out behind them in a strong jet, pushing them forward through the water. When danger threatens, queen scallops can shoot backward rapidly to escape.

The streamlined shape of the shell cuts through the water easily. This means that the scallop can quickly swim away from a lurking starfish.

These ridges running across the shell can tell you how old the scallop is.

About 20 broad ribs fan out from the bottom of the shell to make it extra strong.

Scallops swim by "clapping" the two parts of their shell.

Starfish like to eat scallops. They are strong enough to pull the two valves apart to reach the soft body inside.

The two valves are joined together with a strong elastic substance, called ligament.

SEAFOOD SUPPER

Queen scallops lie on the seafloor with their shells open, waiting for food to float past. They trap tiny plants, called algae, in the waving hairs on their gills. These hairs work like a sieve to filter food from the water.

Barnacles often grow on top of scallop shells. They help disguise the scallops as they lie on the seabed.

FACT FILE
Name Queen scallop
Chalamys opercularis
Size Shell 3.5 in wide
Distribution North western
Europe

A WRINKLY QUEEN
As the soft body of the queen scallop
grows, its shell gets bigger, too. The
speed at which the shell grows
depends on certain things, such as
changes in temperature. This
speeding up and slowing down
causes ridges on the shell, which are
sort of like the rings in a tree trunk.
The more ridges you count, the older
the scallop. Queen scallops can live
for up to eight years.

These tiny,
sensitive
tentacles can
detect enemies,
such as starfish.

These rows of
small, simple
eyes can detect
moving objects
and changes in
light and dark.

The mottled colors of the
shell blend in with the sand
and gravel. This makes it
difficult for enemies, such as
seabirds, to spot the scallop.

LESSER WEEVER FISH

IN CLEAR, SHALLOW water close to the shore, the lesser weever fish lies waiting for a meal to pass by. It often lies almost completely buried, with just its eyes, mouth, and poisonous dorsal fin poking out of the sand or shingle. This means that the fish can see, catch food, and defend itself while most of its body is hidden. In summer, the weever fish moves up and down the shore as the tide goes in and out. It spends winter in deeper waters, farther out to sea, where it can avoid the rough waves that bad weather brings to the coast. The female weever spawns (lays her eggs) in summer. Each tiny egg has a number of yellow oil droplets inside, which keep it from sinking. After about ten days, the eggs hatch into young that float in the sea with the plankton. When the young are fully developed, they leave the surface of the ocean and swim down to the seafloor.

STINGING FINS
If the weever is alarmed or attacked by an enemy, such as a flatfish, it raises its spiny dorsal fin. At the base of these spines there are sacs of poison. If the weever needs to defend itself, it injects poison into the enemy through its sharp spines.

Mottled yellow and brown colors on the body blend in with the seafloor. This helps the fish hide from enemies and prey.

SANDY SECRETS
The weever fish digs itself a shallow dip in the seabed with the fins at the front of its body. It also blows sand out of the way with the water that passes out of its gills. Then it lies in wait, ready to ambush prey, such as shrimp, shore crabs, and worms.

This long fin along the back is supported by about 25 bony rays. There is a similar fin underneath the body.

These pectoral fins are for pushing and steering the fish through the water. They also dig holes in the seabed.

FACT FILE
Name Lesser weever fish
Trachinus vipera
Size 4.5 in long
Distribution Europe and
North America

WATER WORKS
Like all fish, the weever breathes through gills. These work like our lungs to take in oxygen from the water. The weever opens and shuts its mouth all the time, drawing in water. Then it forces the water out again past the gills and the bony gill covers on each side of its head.

Overlapping scales cover and protect the body. They are thin, light, and flexible, so the fish can move easily.

The large mouth sweeps upward out of the sand and gravel to catch food. It also gulps down water for breathing.

Spines on this small black fin inject poison into attackers. The poison runs along grooves in the spines.

A bony cover, called the operculum, protects the delicate gills underneath.

SEAWEEDS

ALL SEAWEEDS BELONG to the algae plant group. They have no flowers, no leaves, and no roots. There are many different kinds of seaweeds, including kelps and bladder wracks. They are divided into three groups – green, brown, and red. Green seaweeds often grow in tide pools high up on the shore, brown seaweeds grow in pools farther down the shore, and red seaweeds grow in the shallow waters around the coast. During a storm, all three kinds are washed up onto the shore and flung into tide pools, where they provide food and shelter for many creatures. Seaweeds reproduce by releasing special male cells that pair up with female cells. These produce spores instead of seeds, and they settle on a rock to grow into a new plant. Many of the young seaweed plants are eaten by mussels, limpets, and other mollusks.

FACT FILE
Name Bladder wrack
Fucus vesiculosus
Size Fronds 4 in long
Distribution Europe and North America

Name Red seaweed
Palmaria palmata
Size 6.5 in long
Distribution Europe and North America

ALGAE ENERGY
Like all plants, seaweeds need light in order to grow. They use the sunlight, together with carbon dioxide and seawater, to make their food. During photosynthesis, seaweeds give off oxygen, which all animals need to survive.

HOLD ON TIGHT
Instead of roots, seaweeds have a holdfast, so-named because it holds on to a rock. It produces a sticky substance called alginic acid, which acts like glue to help it hold on. The holdfast grips the rock so tightly that sometimes strong waves can break off the stipe (stalk), leaving just a stump and the holdfast behind.

Seaweeds contain a green pigment called chlorophyll, that they need for photosynthesis.

This bladder wrack may grow to be more than three feet long.

The stipe is very tough and rubbery. Only the roughest waves can break it.

These parts contain the male and female reproductive cells.

The holdfast supports the stalklike stipe.

FLOATING FRONDS

The round bubbles on this bladder wrack seaweed are called air bladders. They work a lot like inflatable water wings, making the leaflike fronds float up to the surface of tide pools toward the sunlight. There they can photosynthesize more easily.

BED AND BREAKFAST

Seaweeds provide shrimps, crabs, fish, and many other creatures with places to hide from predators. In summer, seaweeds also help block out bright sunlight, which can make the water too hot for the animals that live there. Many kinds of animals feed on seaweeds, including sea slugs and snails.

Air bladders filled with gas keep the leafy fronds floating near the surface of the water.

Seaweeds produce a slimy mucus that stops them from getting too dry when the tide goes out.

This bladder wrack belongs to the group of brown seaweeds.

The pigment in this seaweed helps it photosynthesize in deep water, where little sunlight gets through.

The mass of fronds makes a good hiding place for a shrimp.

All plants contain chlorophyll, but this brown seaweed contains other color pigments as well.

These two feathery tentacles can feel things. The sea lemon uses them to find its food.

SEA LEMON

THE SEA LEMON CREEPS slowly around a tide pool, searching for food. Sea lemons are sea slugs, related to whelks and other mollusks. A sea lemon moves by using the flat, muscular foot on the underside of its body. It feeds on a simple, plantlike animal called a breadcrumb sponge, which grows on rocks and under seaweed. Sea lemons use their radula to scrape food off the rocks. They are hermaphrodites (both male and female at the same time), so any two can mate and lay eggs. These eggs hatch into larvae in the summer. They swim in the open sea for several weeks, then settle on the bottom to turn into tiny adults. They feed and grow among the rocks until spring, when they reach their full size and are ready to mate.

This sea lemon has pulled its gills back inside the body so that you cannot see them at all. This protects them from any damage.

The knobby skin and patchy coloring help disguise the sea lemon.

SNEAKY SLUG
A sea lemon has no shell to protect its soft body. Instead, it is well disguised with its mottled colors and warty skin. The sea lemon's coloring helps it blend in with the pebbles and sand, and hide from its enemies. When a sea lemon keeps absolutely still, it is very difficult to spot in a tide pool.

FACT FILE
Name Sea lemon
Archidoris pseudoargus
Size 2 in long
Distribution Europe

EGGY RIBBON
A sea lemon lays its eggs in a long ribbonlike coil. It glues one end onto a rock using mucus, which it produces inside its body. There may be more than 500,000 eggs in one ribbon. Sea lemons have to lay such a large number because so many of their eggs and larvae are eaten by fish long before they develop into adults.

FRILLY GILLS
The anus on the sea lemon's back is where waste products leave the body. This opening is surrounded by a ring of lacy gills that can move in and out of the body. The sea lemon uses these gills for breathing. Some kinds of sea slugs have no gills, and they breathe through their skin instead.

The outer skin covering the upper part of the body is the sea lemon's mantle.

There is a ring of frilly gills on the back for breathing.

OYSTERCATCHER

ITS LOUD, PIPING CALL and black-and-white pied feathers make the oystercatcher easy to find on the shoreline. As the name suggests, oystercatchers feed mainly on oysters and other mollusks, but they also eat small crabs, shrimps, and worms. In autumn and winter, these birds live in large groups, called flocks. In spring and summer, they form pairs and find a small territory on the shore where they lay their eggs. A female lays two to four eggs in a shallow hole, called a scrape. The male and female take turns sitting on the eggs, which hatch after about four weeks. The chicks can run around soon after hatching, but they rely on their parents to feed them for several weeks, or even months.

FACT FILE
Name Oystercatcher
Haematopus ostralegus
Size 17 in long
Distribution North western Africa, Europe, India, the Middle East, and Scandinavia

SPOT THE EGG
The colors and patterns on the oystercatcher's eggs make them look like pebbles, so they are difficult for enemies to spot. Oystercatchers sometimes try to fool an enemy by getting off their eggs and pretending to sit on them somewhere else.

The nostrils are high up, so they do not become clogged with sand when the bird is digging for food.

The tip of the bill is narrow and strong, for prying the two halves of a shell apart.

This joint looks like a knee, but it is really an ankle.

The feet spread wide so that the oystercatcher does not sink as it walks on wet sand.

The speckled eggs blend in well with the pebbles, which makes it difficult for enemies to find them.

A SMASHING BILL

An oystercatcher's long, blunt bill is specially adapted for breaking open shells. It levers them off rocks, and pries or smashes them open. When the bird finds an open shell, it pushes its bill between the two halves and cuts the muscle that holds them together. If the shell is closed, the bird hammers away at one side with its bill until it breaks through to the soft flesh inside.

A thick covering of waterproof feathers on the body keeps it warm and dry.

NOISY NEIGHBORS

During breeding season, oystercatchers become very noisy, as each pair claims its own territory on the shore. All the birds rush around with their bills pointing down toward the ground, making shrill piping calls. These loud messages warn other birds to keep away.

The tail feathers help the oystercatcher to steer in the air. They also balance the weight of the bird's body when it perches or sits on the ground.

SHARING THE SHORE

An oystercatcher is just one of the many kinds of birds that poke around on the shoreline looking for food. Each kind of bird has a different size or shape of bill so that it can find food at different depths in the mud or sand. In this way, the birds share the rich food supply, and many different kinds of birds can live close together.

DOG WHELK

THE CARNIVOROUS dog whelk creeps slowly over rocks, hunting for its food. It feeds on mussels, barnacles, and limpets. Whelks are a type of snail and they belong to the group of animals called mollusks. They build shells to protect their soft bodies, using chalk from the water. In spring and autumn, dog whelks gather together to mate. The females lay oval-shaped capsules in cracks in the rock, and each capsule contains hundreds of eggs. After four months, tiny whelks hatch out. They shelter from the waves in crevices until they are almost a half-inch long. Then they leave the safety of the rocks and begin to hunt for themselves.

SOFT CENTERS

Like whelks, mussels are mollusks, with soft bodies inside hard shells. But mussel shells have two halves, called valves, which can open and close when the mussel feeds.

This pale-colored dog whelk has been eating the tiny barnacles covering the rock.

This bright orange layer on the rock is a simple animal called a sponge.

UNUSUAL CUTLERY

To feed, the dog whelk pushes a hollow tube called a proboscis between the two valves of a mussel. Then it scrapes out the flesh inside with its radula. The radula can also bore holes through shells with the help of a special chemical that the dog whelk produces to soften them. Drilling the hole can take as long as three days.

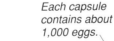

Each capsule contains about 1,000 eggs.

EGG EATERS

During the breeding season, a female dog whelk lays about 10 egg capsules. Each capsule may take up to an hour to lay, and measures about a quarter-inch long. Only 20 to 30 of the eggs inside each capsule are fertile (able to develop). They survive by eating the other eggs. When this happens, the capsules begin to turn purple.

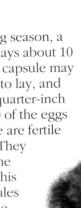

This dog whelk has just found its next meal of mussels.

FACT FILE
Name Dog whelk
        Nucella lapillus
Size Shell 1 in long
Distribution Europe and North and South America

PICK A COLOR
Dog whelks can be all sorts of colors, including yellow, pink, orange, and purple. You can tell what a dog whelk feeds on by the color of its shell. Pale-colored dog whelks have eaten barnacles, and dark-colored whelks have fed on mussels. Some whelks, such as this one, have banded shells. Scientists think this may be due to a varied diet.

As a dog whelk grows bigger, it builds up the open end of its shell.

Inside this tube is the proboscis, which the dog whelk uses to feed and breathe.

The tip of the shell is called the apex.

SEA URCHINS

THESE UNUSUAL CREATURES look more like prickly tennis balls than living animals, but they are closely related to starfish. Sea urchins and starfish belong to the group of animals called *Echinodermata*, which means "spiny-skinned." Like starfish, sea urchins move around using their special tube feet. They can climb up steep rocks, and cling on tightly when waves splash over them. Despite being covered in sharp spines, sea urchins are sometimes attacked by predators, such as fish. To disguise themselves, they use their tube feet to pick up bits of seaweed and attach them to their spines. Sea urchins release their eggs into the water in the spring. The fertilized eggs develop into tiny larvae. These float around among the plankton and eventually settle down on the seafloor or in a tide pool to grow into adults.

FACT FILE
Name Sea urchins
Lytechnicus species
Size 2.5 in wide
Distribution Europe and North and South America

GREEDY GRAZER

Sea urchins are omnivores (plant and meat eaters). They graze on tiny plants and animals in tide pools using the mouth on the underside of their body. The mouth has five powerful, toothlike plates for scraping food off rocks. Inside, it is shaped like an old-fashioned lantern. Sea urchins are sometimes called "Aristotle's lanterns," after the Ancient Greek who first wrote about them.

Sea urchins can be all sorts of colors. They often match their surroundings, as this one does.

The mouth is at the base of the body, so the sea urchin can feed as it moves along.

A TOUGH TEST

A sea urchin's outer skeleton is also called a test. It is made up of plates, which grow larger as the animal grows. These plates touch one another and make the test very strong. Its surface is covered with rows of sharp spines. They wave around as the water flows over them, so they do not snap off easily.

The spines are made of chalk. Each one can move without the others.

PERFECT ARMOR

Sea urchins are well-protected by their long spines. These are in rows, and between them are the tube feet. Some of the spines have pincerlike ends. If the sea urchin is attacked by a predator, these special pincers break off and stick in the attacker's skin, where they inject poison. The spines and pincers can regenerate (regrow) over and over again.

The sharp spines are in rows from top to bottom.

At the top is the anus, where waste materials leave the body.

Close up, you can see the tube feet waving around.

These special pincers can inject an attacker with poison.

STARFISH

WHEN THE TIDE IS OUT, starfish and their relatives, brittle stars, hide under rocks. But when the tide comes in they leave the shelter of the rocks to search for food. Starfish are predators and eat mussels and other shelled creatures. They pry open shells with their strong arms, then turn their stomachs inside out over their victims to digest the animals inside. Brittle stars trap small, soft-bodied creatures between the spines on their arms, then pass the food on to their mouths. In spring and summer, starfish and brittle stars release millions of eggs into the water. The fertilized eggs develop into larvae, which float in the sea for about three weeks, then settle on the bottom of a tide pool to grow into adults.

FACT FILE
Name Scarlet serpent brittle star *Ophioderma* species
Size Arms 6 in long
Distribution Australia, the Caribbean, and Europe

Name Spiny starfish *Marthasterias glacialis*
Size 4.5 in wide
Distribution Europe

Brittle stars only use their tube feet for passing food down to the mouth.

These rows of spines are part of the brittle star's skeleton.

The mouth is on the underside of the body.

A brittle star's arms grow all the time. If part of an arm is pulled off, the arm simply grows from the broken end.

These little spines trap all sorts of food, including small shrimps.

Few predators risk these sharp spines for such a light snack.

The brittle star wriggles its arms vigorously from side to side to move itself along.

BRITTLE ARMS

Brittle stars have special bony plates in their arms that allow them to move from side to side extremely quickly, but not up and down. A brittle star's arms are very brittle indeed, and they can break off easily. If an arm gets broken off, a new one soon grows in its place. This is called regeneration.

SPINY SKELETONS

Starfish have skeletons made of chalk inside their bodies. But parts of the skeleton also stick out of the skin, like little spines. These spines sometimes have tiny pincers on them for cleaning the arms. Starfish and brittle stars belong to the group of animals called *Echinodermata*.

Starfish have suckers on their tube feet that help them to grip onto rocks.

The starfish uses its strong tube feet for walking.

This spiny starfish has a ring of tiny pincers around each spine for cleaning its arms.

Starfish grasp prey with their strong arms.

TRAVELING BY TUBE

Starfish and brittle stars have tube feet on the undersides of their arms. Brittle stars use these to push food into their mouths, but they cannot use them for moving around, as starfish can. Each tube foot is full of fluid. Muscles pump the fluid in and out of the feet to move them up and down. This is how a starfish walks, and how a brittle star feeds itself.

The brilliant color of this scarlet serpent brittle star makes it easy to spot.

These pink tips are simple eyes. They can sense light and darkness.

SEA SCORPION

AMONG THE SEAWEED in deep tide pools, sea scorpions lurk, waiting to gobble up smaller fish and shrimps. These fish cannot swim fast, but they have huge mouths, so they manage to catch plenty to eat. This short-spined sea scorpion can grow up to one foot long. Its mottled coloring helps it hide from enemies as well as from its prey. Sea scorpions breed in winter and early spring. The females lay a mass of orange eggs, often in a crevice between the rocks. Sometimes a male digs a hollow in the bottom of the tide pool and the female lays her eggs there. The male usually guards the eggs until they hatch into tiny larvae. These swim among the plankton, and finally grow into fish in early summer.

FACT FILE
Name Short-spined sea scorpion *Myoxocephalus scorpius*
Size 4 in long
Distribution Europe and North America

MANY NAMES

This fish is also called a bull rout, sting-fish, or father-lasher. All these names give you an idea of its fierce behavior. Sea scorpions sometimes drive away much larger fish, including sharks, from their hunting grounds. They twist their bodies quickly in the water, so that their sharp spines whip around toward the enemy and frighten it off.

Each large eye can swivel in its socket to see all around.

These short spines protect the protruding eyes.

These two holes are nostrils, called nares. The fish uses them for smelling.

Each fin is made of long bones with skin stretched between them, like the webbed foot of a duck.

The mouth opens very wide, so smaller fish can be swallowed in one gulp.

Waste material leaves the body through this hole, called the anal vent.

The two pelvic fins are close together on the underside. They help support the heavy head when the fish is resting on a rock.

The fish uses the caudal fin for steering.

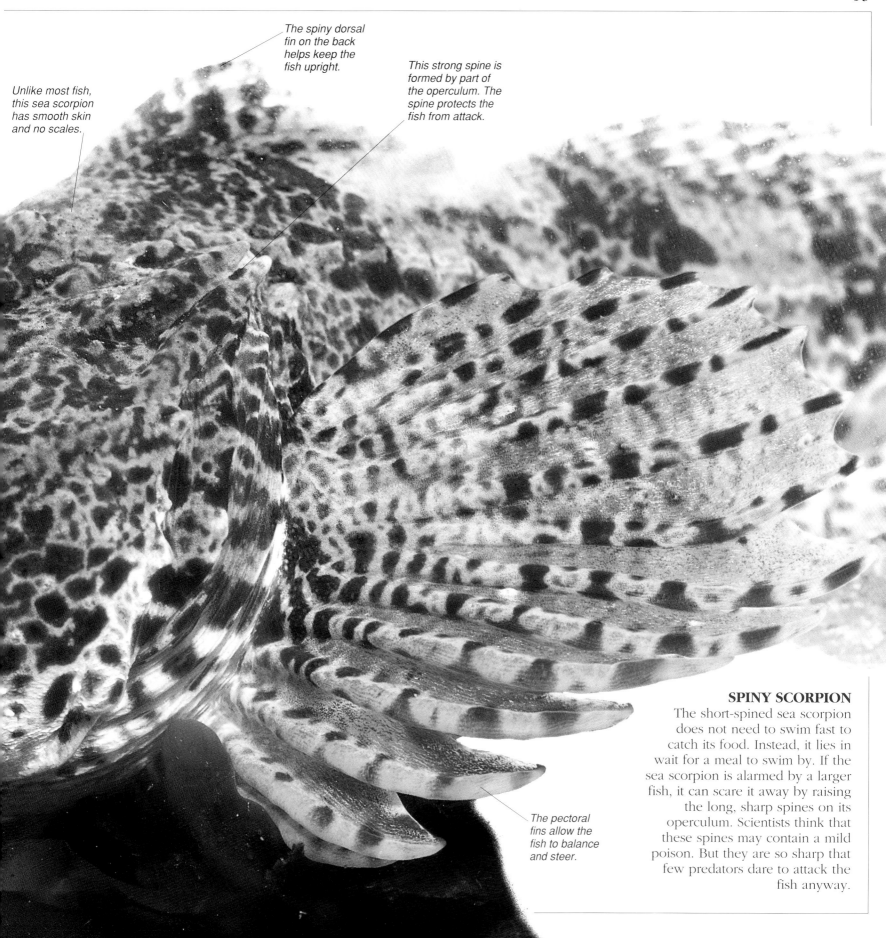

The spiny dorsal fin on the back helps keep the fish upright.

This strong spine is formed by part of the operculum. The spine protects the fish from attack.

Unlike most fish, this sea scorpion has smooth skin and no scales.

The pectoral fins allow the fish to balance and steer.

SPINY SCORPION

The short-spined sea scorpion does not need to swim fast to catch its food. Instead, it lies in wait for a meal to swim by. If the sea scorpion is alarmed by a larger fish, it can scare it away by raising the long, sharp spines on its operculum. Scientists think that these spines may contain a mild poison. But they are so sharp that few predators dare to attack the fish anyway.

PIECRUST CRABS

THESE CRABS ARE well named, because the top part of their shell, the carapace, looks just like the pastry lid of a pie. These crabs spend much of their time hiding under rocks or seaweed, and they are much less aggressive than their relatives, the velvet crabs. Piecrust crabs eat shellfish, such as shrimps and mussels. They are also great scavengers, eating the remains of dead creatures that they find in tide pools. Adult piecrust crabs can grow to measure more than six inches across the shell. The little crabs that you see in tide pools are still very young. As they grow, they move down the shore into deeper water. A piecrust crab can live for eight years or more, but the female does not lay eggs until she is about five years old. She may lay more than three million eggs during her lifetime, but only a few will survive to grow into adults.

FACT FILE
Name Piecrust (or edible) crab
Cancer pagurus
Size Shell 4 in wide
Distribution Europe

RAISING THE ROOF
The crab's body is well protected by its exoskeleton. Like shrimps, lobsters, and other crustaceans, the crab molts its exoskeleton every few weeks as it grows, revealing a new one underneath. To get out of the old shell, the crab swallows so much water that the top part of the shell is forced away from the bottom part. The crab then pulls itself out backward.

The fluted edge of the carapace makes this crab look like a piecrust, so it is easy to recognize.

The hard exoskeleton is colored and patterned to blend in well with the pebbles on the beach.

Huge, blunt pincers with serrated (notched) edges grasp food.

Joints on each leg allow the crab to move easily and scuttle away quickly to hide from enemies.

The crab's sharp claws provide it with extra grip for scrambling over rocks.

The setae helps the crab to feel its way around.

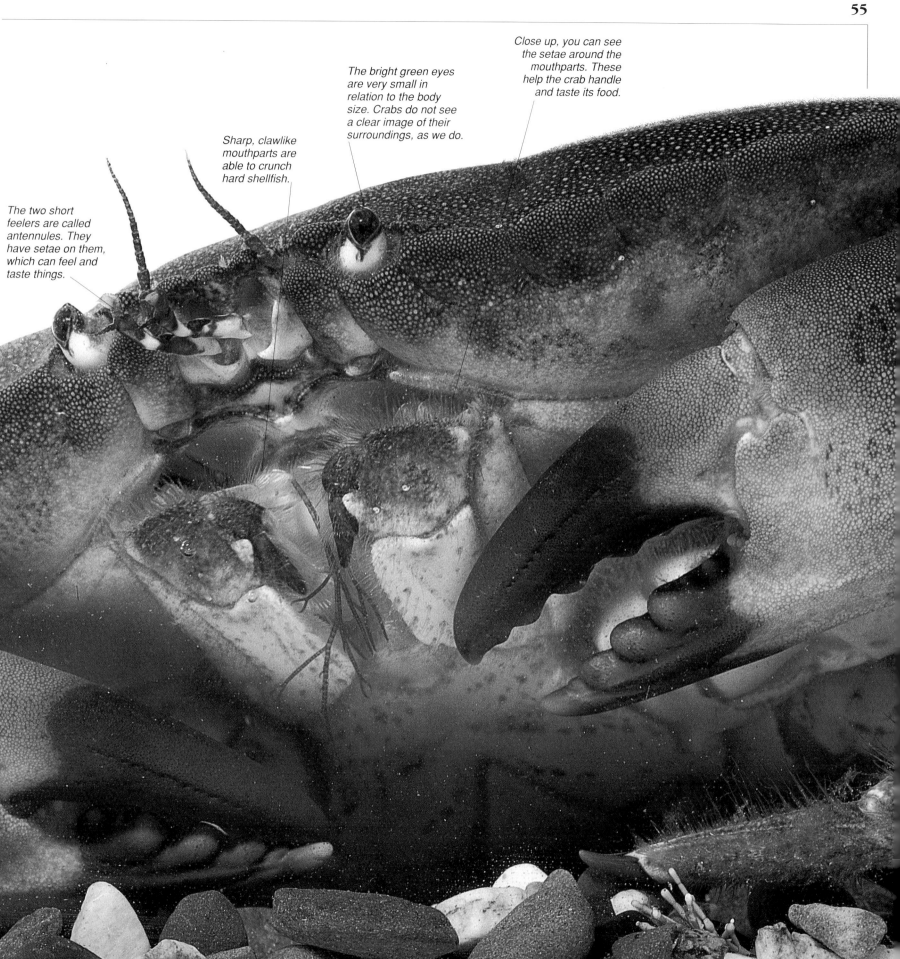

Close up, you can see the setae around the mouthparts. These help the crab handle and taste its food.

The bright green eyes are very small in relation to the body size. Crabs do not see a clear image of their surroundings, as we do.

Sharp, clawlike mouthparts are able to crunch hard shellfish.

The two short feelers are called antennules. They have setae on them, which can feel and taste things.

SEA ANEMONES

THESE CREATURES MAY look like harmless flowers, but they are carnivorous animals. Sea anemones are related to jellyfish and, like them, most have stinging tentacles to paralyze victims. The sea anemone waits for prey (such as a fish) to swim by, then stings it with its tentacles, and pushes it into its mouth opening. Sea anemones spend most of their lives in one place, attached to rocks or buried in mud. Sometimes they divide themselves in two to make a second anemone. They can also make dozens of tiny copies of themselves, which swim out through the mouth opening. Other kinds of anemones produce minute, slipper-shaped larvae, and these swim away to begin their lives elsewhere.

FACT FILE
Name Snakelocks anemone
Anemonia sulcata
Size 1.25 in high
Distribution Europe and North America

Name Strawberry anemone
Actinia fragacea
Size 2.75 in high
Distribution England and France

Name Beadlet anemone
Actinia equina
Size 2.75 in high
Distribution Europe and North America

FAT STRAWBERRY
A strawberry anemone is similar in color and shape to a plump, ripe strawberry. Each time it eats a meal, its body becomes very fat and round. Its tentacles almost disappear inside the body, and they stay there until the anemone needs to eat again.

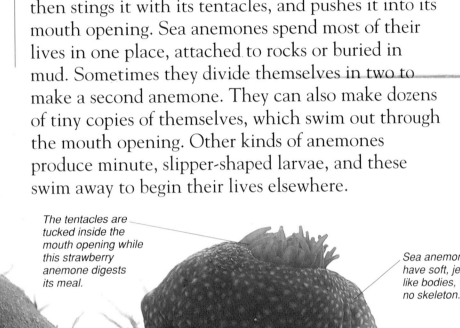

The tentacles are tucked inside the mouth opening while this strawberry anemone digests its meal.

Sea anemones have soft, jelly-like bodies, with no skeleton.

A suckerlike disk under the column holds on to the rock so tightly that the waves cannot knock the anemone off.

The tentacles wave gently in the current.

This part of the body is called the column.

STINGING SNAKES

Snakelocks anemones hardly ever draw their tentacles back into their bodies. They wave around most of the time, waiting for prey such as small shrimps to brush against them. Fully grown snakelocks anemones have about 200 tentacles, which can measure up to six inches long. Their sting is too mild to hurt a human, and just feels sticky to our touch.

BEADS AND BLOBS

When the tide goes out, beadlet anemones look like small blobs of jelly clinging to the rocks. These anemones are so-named because there is a ring of 24 blue or mauve beadlets, containing extra-strong stinging cells, around the base of the tentacles. The anemone's tentacles do not sting other anemones, but if it is attacked by one of its own kind, the beadlets swell up so that it can use them to defend itself.

During low tide, this beadlet anemone tucks its tentacles inside its body. This prevents it from losing too much precious water.

Close up, you can just see the row of poisonous, mauve beads underneath the tentacles.

Dozens of tentacles surround the mouth to help push prey into the opening.

These pink tips may warn enemies that the tentacles are poisonous.

Each tentacle of this snakelocks anemone is armed with stinging cells.

This beadlet anemone is slowly digesting a small fish that it has caught.

KING RAGWORMS

THESE COLORFUL WORMS get their name from the ragged fringe of flat legs, called parapodia, along the sides of their bodies. Ragworms often live in burrows beneath the surface of the sand, and they wriggle around to keep a current of water flowing past. Water contains oxygen, which a ragworm needs in order to breathe. When the ragworm senses prey, it shoots out of its burrow to grab it. In the breeding season, female king ragworms lay eggs on the seabed, and the males fertilize them. Then all the adults die. Their eggs develop into tiny larvae that swim around, feeding on plankton, while they grow and develop. After about two years, they will be fully grown adults, living in the sand.

FACT FILE
Name King ragworm
Nereis virens
Size 1 ft long
Distribution North eastern Asia, northern Europe, and North America

TINY TENTACLES
Each body segment has a pair of flat, paddlelike parapodia. The ragworm uses these for crawling, swimming, and breathing. They work like the gills of a fish to take in oxygen from the water. Each one has two small, feelerlike cirri and two bundles of stiff bristles, for gripping surfaces.

These iridescent violet colors are made by light reflecting off both sides of the worm's thin skin.

The body is made up of more than 100 segments.

FOOD FINDERS

On the ragworm's head there are many sense organs. These help it hunt for food and pick up information about its environment. The four eyes, two palps, and two antennae are sensitive to light, smell, and touch. There are also four tentacles that can feel things.

These two short antennae, and the two palps, help the worm find food. The mouth is on the underside of the head.

If king ragworms lose their tentacles, they can grow new ones.

SHRINKING WORM

To escape from enemies, such as birds, the king ragworm contracts (tightens) the muscles that run from its head to its tail. This makes its body much shorter, so the ragworm can move backward suddenly, or disappear into its burrow quickly.

PINCER POWER

The king ragworm is an omnivore, eating almost anything that it can find. This animal is a fierce hunter, seizing prey with its strong, pincerlike jaws. There are six to ten teeth on each jaw.

The bristles on the parapodia can spread out like a fan to help the worm grip the sand and mud.

The worm's body is flat, so it can crawl into cracks and under stones, and slide through the sand easily.

SHANNIES AND ROCKLINGS

THESE FISH SPEND ALMOST all of their lives in tide pools, where they feed on shrimps, prawns, and small crabs. They are agile swimmers, and can dart away quickly if they are disturbed. Their coloring helps them blend in well with the seaweed, and keeps them safe from birds and other predators. In the spring and summer, shannies lay eggs under rocks or in crevices. The male guards the eggs for about eight weeks until they hatch. Shannies only leave the shore during the winter, when they move into deeper water to avoid being thrown against the rocks by rough tides. Rocklings leave their tide pools in early spring to lay their eggs out at sea. The eggs float in the water and gradually develop into larvae, then young fish, which swim ashore to find their own tide pool homes.

FISH FOR DINNER
Young rocklings swim together in huge groups, called schools. These schools of tiny fish provide larger fish, such as mackerel, with a tasty meal. Young rocklings are sometimes nicknamed mackerel midge. Those that survive to grow into adults swim ashore to tide pools in the summer.

SMOOTH SHANNY
Shannies do not have scales covering their bodies, so they are very smooth and slippery. This, together with their long, streamlined body shape, enables them to slip easily between rocks and under seaweed to find food or hide from enemies.

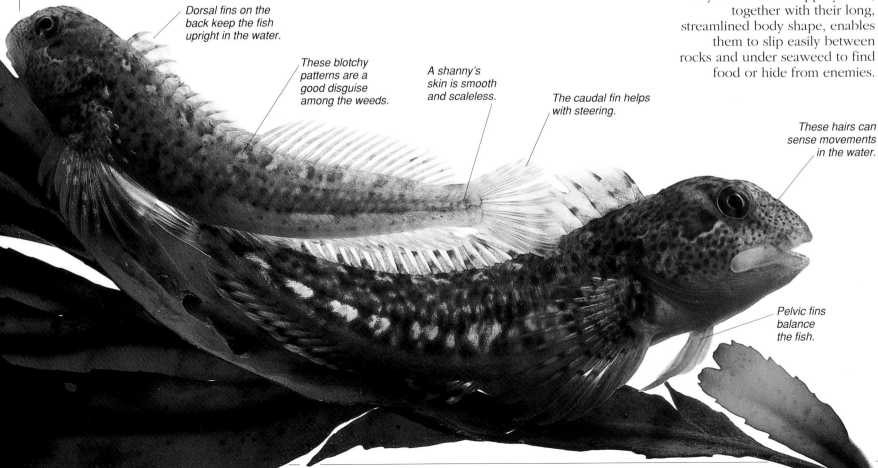

Dorsal fins on the back keep the fish upright in the water.

These blotchy patterns are a good disguise among the weeds.

A shanny's skin is smooth and scaleless.

The caudal fin helps with steering.

These hairs can sense movements in the water.

Pelvic fins balance the fish.

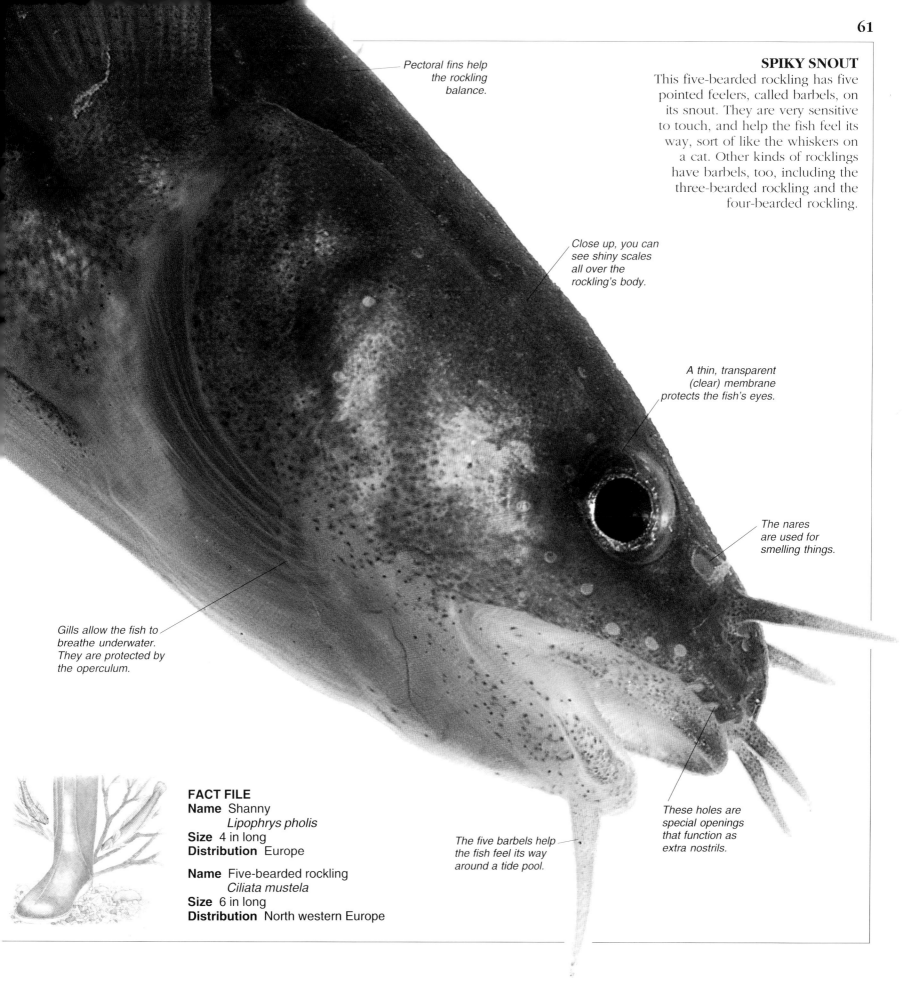

Pectoral fins help the rockling balance.

SPIKY SNOUT
This five-bearded rockling has five pointed feelers, called barbels, on its snout. They are very sensitive to touch, and help the fish feel its way, sort of like the whiskers on a cat. Other kinds of rocklings have barbels, too, including the three-bearded rockling and the four-bearded rockling.

Close up, you can see shiny scales all over the rockling's body.

A thin, transparent (clear) membrane protects the fish's eyes.

The nares are used for smelling things.

Gills allow the fish to breathe underwater. They are protected by the operculum.

These holes are special openings that function as extra nostrils.

FACT FILE
Name Shanny
   Lipophrys pholis
Size 4 in long
Distribution Europe

Name Five-bearded rockling
   Ciliata mustela
Size 6 in long
Distribution North western Europe

The five barbels help the fish feel its way around a tide pool.

VELVET CRAB

THE COLORFUL VELVET CRAB is one of the most ferocious of all crabs. Its bright red eyes and sharp blue pincers make it look very fierce indeed. Velvet crabs are aggressive predators, and eat almost anything that they can find in tide pools and on the shore. If a velvet crab is threatened, it rears up on its back legs and holds its sharp pincers out. This makes it look bigger and should frighten its enemy away. If the crab loses a claw in battle, a new one usually grows to replace it. This new claw can be even bigger than the original one. Like all crabs, velvet crabs reproduce by laying eggs. These develop into larvae, and about five weeks later they turn into tiny crabs. An adult female lays millions of eggs during her lifetime, although most of her young will be eaten by fish long before they can grow into crabs.

Strong mouthparts can chew even shellfish.

Close up, you can see masses of tiny eggs on the underside of this crab's body.

This flap, formed by the abdomen, keeps the mass of eggs in place.

POWERFUL PADDLER

Velvet crabs are strong swimmers. Their unusual paddle-shaped back legs help them swim away extra fast to escape from predators, such as gulls. These special legs also give velvet crabs their other name of "swimming crabs."

VELVET COAT

The velvet crab is so-named because its carapace is covered with fine, velvety hairs. Silt (fine pieces of sand) becomes trapped in these hairs, giving the crab its muddy gray color. This coloring is a good disguise when the crab is resting on the sandy bottom of a tide pool.

The last joint of the back leg is flattened, so it looks like a paddle.

A layer of velvety hairs covers the carapace.

Sharp, toothlike spikes on the pincers make them even more deadly.

OODLES OF EGGS

This female crab is carrying thousands of eggs under her body. The abdomen forms a special flap that holds the eggs in place. After about three months, they hatch into tiny larvae, called zoea. These swim in the open sea among the plankton for several weeks before they begin to change into crabs.

Antennae on the head help the crab find its way around, even in the dark.

The antennules are used for tasting things

Each pincer is pointed, with serrated edges for crushing and cutting up food.

These beady red eyes scare away predators and warn them not to attack.

This row of sharp spikes helps protect the crab from enemies. The spikes are so sharp that it is difficult to pick the crab up.

Silt is trapped between all these fine hairs.

If one of the legs breaks off, a new one will soon grow to replace it.

Joints allow the legs to bend.

FACT FILE
Name Velvet crab
Liocarcinus puber
Size Shell 2.75 in wide
Distribution Europe and North Africa

SEA PEAS AND THRIFT

IN SUMMER, SEA PEAS and thrift bring patches of bright color to the shoreline. These plants grow among the rocks and pebbles on the shore and are able to survive the salty spray blowing in from the sea. Many shoreline plants, such as thrift and sea peas, have long roots to reach the rainwater that trickles between the pebbles and collects underground. These plants grow low on the ground, out of the wind. But thrift flowers have long stems, so when the wind blows, it shakes out the seeds. They fall to the ground and grow into new plants somewhere else along the shore.

LEAFY CUSHIONS

The leaves of thrift grow in a low, grasslike cushion. Close to the ground, the plant can survive the constant buffeting of sea winds. The cushion also traps moisture, so any water vapor that escapes from the leaves is less likely to be blown away by the wind.

FACT FILE
Name Sea pea *Lathyrus japonicus (maritimus)*
Size Flower 0.5 in wide, stem 4 in long
Distribution North America, northern Asia, and northern Europe

FUNNY FLOWER
A sea pea flower is an unusual shape. It has a large petal at the top and a smaller one on either side. There are two more petals at the bottom that protect the pollen sacs and the female parts of the flower.

Sea pea flowers look similar to sweet pea flowers.

Each flower head is made up of several flowers at the top of a long, hairy stalk.

Paper-thin sepals and delicate, leaf-like bracts protect each flower.

FACT FILE
Name Thrift
Armeria maritima
Size Flower 0.5 in wide, stem 3.5 in long
Distribution North of the Equator

GETTING A GRIP

Thrift roots can grow to more than three feet long, and the creeping stems of a sea pea plant can be up to 31 inches long. This helps the plants to stay firmly anchored to the ground in bad weather conditions.

Thrift plants are also called sea pinks.

The thrift's narrow leaves grow close to the ground, where they are protected from the wind.

The five pollen sacs are at the center of each flower.

NATTERJACK TOAD

FACT FILE
Name Natterjack toad
Bufo calamita
Size 2.5 in long
Distribution Europe

DURING THE DAY, the natterjack toad stays inside its sandy burrow. When night falls, the toad creeps out of its hiding place to hunt for insects in the cool, damp air. Natterjack toads hibernate (sleep) during the cold winter months, burying themselves deep in the sand. In spring they migrate to fresh water nearby, where they breed. The males croak loudly to attract females. After mating, the females lay strings of eggs about six feet long in the water. Each string may contain up to 4,000 eggs. Five to ten days later, tadpoles hatch out of the eggs and swim around, feeding mainly on algae. After six to eight weeks they have changed into tiny toads measuring less than a half inch long. Now they are ready to leave the water and begin life on the shore. It will take four or five years for these young toads to become fully grown.

HUNGRY HUNTER
Natterjack toads feed mainly on insects, especially ants and beetles. They have huge appetites, and may eat hundreds of insects in one night. The toad flicks out its tongue at an insect, catching it on the sticky tip. As the toad swallows the prey, it blinks. This forces its eyes down into the head, and helps push food down the throat.

PEELING OFF
The natterjack toad breathes with its lungs, and also through its skin. So it is important that the skin stays in good condition. Like frogs and other amphibians, the toad molts every five or six days. It peels off the old skin with its mouth and front feet, to reveal a shiny new skin underneath. Natterjack toads usually eat their old skin.

LITTLE LEGS
Natterjack toads have much shorter back legs than most other toads and frogs. They cannot swim or jump as well as their relatives, but they are surprisingly nimble, and are good at walking and running.

Natterjack toads are sometimes called golden backs because of this narrow yellow line along the back.

Bulging eyes give the toad a wide field of vision.

The nostrils are used to take air into the lungs.

Strong front legs are used for burrowing into sand.

Short back legs can walk and run quickly.

The toes are webbed and widely splayed. This is a good shape for shoveling sand.

DO NOT DISTURB

If the natterjack toad spots a predator, such as a bird, it can puff up its body and straighten its back legs to make itself look taller, fatter, and fiercer. This is often enough to stop the animal from attacking the toad. But if a predator does grab it, a foul-tasting poison oozes out from the parotid glands behind its eyes. Most animals quickly drop the toad and look for a tastier meal instead.

A round, flat eardrum on each side of the head picks up sounds.

These large lumps are parotid glands full of poison, which oozes out if an enemy attacks the toad.

Patterns and bumps on the skin help the toad blend in with its sandy surroundings.

FIDDLER CRABS

AS THE TIDE GOES OUT, a shoreline of tangled roots and sticky mud is uncovered. Suddenly, dozens of fiddler crabs like these pop out of their burrows and scuttle around in search of food. They are scavengers, feeding on small particles of food, such as algae, on the surface of the shore. When danger threatens, they dash back into their burrows for safety. Some fiddler crabs also live in the mud of swamps, and some live in sand banks. Each crab has its own territory. The territories are very small, because there are so many other fiddler crabs sharing the shore. Male fiddler crabs have one small pincer and one enormous one. They use the giant pincer to signal to females, and to scare other males away from their territory.

FACT FILE
Name Fiddler crab
Uca vocans
Size Shell 0.5 in wide
Distribution Africa, southern Asia, Australia, India, and Indonesia

A CLASH OF CLAWS
If two males confront each other, the smaller one is usually wise enough to retreat. Even two well-matched males settle most arguments simply by threatening each other with their claws. But if this fails, then a real fight breaks out. The crabs lock their large pincers together and wrestle until one of them gives in.

Inside each pincer there are strong muscles that open and shut it, so that the crab can hold on tightly to the claw of another male fiddler crab.

The crab's right claw is usually the larger one.

SPRINTING SIDEWAYS
Crabs have four pairs of long legs arranged along a wide, but short body. They can walk forward slowly, but each leg can only take a short step without tripping over the leg in front. By stepping sideways, the legs can take much bigger strides. When crabs are startled, they can run sideways very fast indeed.

MUD PIE
These crabs are good at getting food out of the mud. They scrape up a ball of mud with their pincers, then pass it to their mouthparts. These roll the ball around while the crab sucks all the nutrients out of it. Afterward, it drops these mud balls near its burrow. The mud balls are called pseudofeces, which means "false droppings."

FLAG-WAVING
The male fiddler crab uses his large pincer much like a flag. He spends a lot of his time waving it proudly at females he hopes to attract. Each kind of fiddler crab waves its claw in a special pattern, so that it only appeals to females of the same kind. This helps avoid confusion, and it is useful in the swamp, where many kinds of fiddler crabs live close together.

The crab's eyes have long stalks that allow it to peep out over the rim of its burrow and watch for danger.

The small pincer gathers food.

The legs are made up of rigid segments, with flexible joints so they can bend.

PEACOCK WORMS

AT LOW TIDE, PEACOCK worms look like tiny, muddy pipes sticking out of the beach. But when the tide comes in and covers them with water, beautiful feathery fans spread out from the ends of each tube. These fans are the gills of peacock worms. A peacock worm's soft body is hidden inside its long, protective tube, which it builds from mud and sand. Each tube sticks up about 4 inches above the shore, but there may be another 16 inches hidden in the sand below. The body is divided into hundreds of segments, like the body of an earthworm. In spring and summer, peacock worms release many tiny eggs into the water. These eggs hatch into larvae that drift in the ocean with the plankton. After about two weeks, they settle down on the shore, where they each build a tube to live in.

FACT FILE
Name Peacock worm
Sabella pavonina
Size Body 10 in long
Distribution Europe

The gills are for breathing, as well as for catching food.

The worm makes its tube from mud and sand, cemented together with slimy mucus.

FOOD FAN
The feathery gills catch tiny water creatures and scraps of food floating past in the water. Each gill pushes food toward the worm's mouth, which is at the center of the fan. The gills also trap tiny particles of sand and mud.

The worm's mouth is hidden in the center of its gills.

The gills sense movements in the water and changes in light and dark.

In times of danger, and when the tide is out, the worm pulls its head and gills back inside the tube.

MUD AND SLIME
A peacock worm builds its smooth, rounded tube out of tiny pieces of mud and fine sand. It sticks them together with mucus, which it makes in its body. The inside of the tube is lined with mucus, so that the worm can slide up and down easily.

Close up, you can see fringes of tiny hairs, called cilia. These help trap food and move it toward the mouth.

The fan is divided into two semicircles. Each of these has between 8 and 45 gills.

The gills can be all sorts of colors, such as brown, red, or purple. They usually have darker bands of color running through them.

LYING LOW
Peacock worms are usually covered by water. When they are exposed to the air at low tide, the worms go right down to the bottom of their tubes. There they stay cool, damp, and safe from enemies.

The lower end of the tube is usually attached to pebbles beneath the sand. This keeps it firmly in place when waves wash over it.

MUDSKIPPER

THE MUDSKIPPER'S NAME fits it perfectly. It spends more time skipping across mudflats than swimming in water. It will even climb up a mangrove tree in search of food. Mudskippers spend most of their time out of the water, but they need to keep their skin moist. When they get too dry, they roll in puddles and wipe their faces with a wet fin. These fish can move much faster on land than in water. They hunt energetically for small creatures, such as insects, to eat. The mudskipper is not sociable, and if another mudskipper gets too close, it warns off the intruder by raising the fin on its back. When danger threatens, the mudskipper dives into the water and hides in the mud among the tangled mangrove roots. During the rainy season, these fish dig burrows in the mud so the females can give birth to their live young in safety.

FANTASTIC FINS
The mudskipper's fins are adapted so that it can walk, jump, swim, and even climb. The pectoral fins look like little arms. The fish uses them for moving around on land. The pelvic fins are shorter and joined together underneath the body to make a kind of sucker. This sucker helps the mudskipper cling onto mangrove roots when it climbs.

POP-UP PEEPERS
The mudskipper's bulging eyes are close together on the top of its head. They stick up so that the fish can see all around itself. When the mudskipper swims, its eyes peep out of the water. They can move up and down like the periscopes of a submarine, and allow the mudskipper to see above and below the water at the same time.

These two fish may look as if they are being friendly, but in fact their dorsal fins are raised in anger.

Mudskippers can breathe through their skin as well as their gills.

When it is out of water, the mudskipper keeps its eyes moist by rolling them back into their sockets every so often.

These mottled colors blend in well with the patches of light and shade in the swamps of tropical shores.

The torpedo-shaped body allows the mudskipper to swim easily through water.

OXYGEN TANKS
Like all fish, the mudskipper breathes with its feathery gills. It waves water over them with its gill covers, and absorbs oxygen from the water into its blood. Before climbing out of the water, the mudskipper fills its large gill chambers with water. These act like oxgyen tanks, keeping the fish's blood supplied with oxygen while it is on land.

The lateral line helps the fish keep its balance in the water.

The upper part of the pectoral fin is strong and muscular to support the fish's weight.

The gill covers shut tight when the mudskipper is on land to store water inside the gill chambers.

This strangely shaped mouth is good for snapping up insects, spiders, and even small crabs.

These sharp teeth can easily grab prey.

Suckerlike pelvic fins help the fish cling to slippery mangrove roots and rocks.

These stiff rays dig into the sand when the fish walks.

FACT FILE
Name Mudskipper
Periophthalmus barbarus
Size 4.25 in long
Distribution Australia, eastern Africa, India, the South Pacific islands, and Southeast Asia

COMMON LIZARDS

THESE COMMON LIZARDS can slip easily through clumps of grass on the shore, hunting for insects and spiders to eat. Like all reptiles, lizards need to be warm in order to move around, and they often stretch out on the sand to bask in the sunshine. Winter is too cold for them, and food is short, so they find a sheltered place, such as a burrow, where they can hibernate. In spring, common lizards form pairs for mating. The female finds a damp place in the sand and lays 4 to 11 eggs, which are protected by a transparent membrane. The young soon emerge and run around, feeding on spiders and insects, such as flies. The adults take little interest in their young, and many of them are eaten by snakes, birds, or mammals.

An eyelid wipes over each eye to keep it clean.

The colors and patterns on the lizard's scales help hide it from both predators and prey.

Like most reptiles, lizards shed their skin in order to grow.

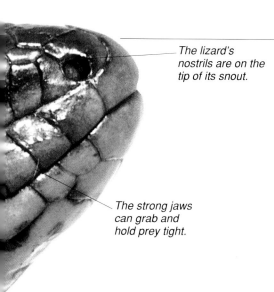

The lizard's nostrils are on the tip of its snout.

The strong jaws can grab and hold prey tight.

SIXTH SENSE

The common lizard belongs to a group of animals called reptiles. Like most animals, reptiles can see, hear, feel, taste, and smell. They also have a forked tongue, which picks up chemical information from the air. A special organ in the roof of the mouth uses the information to build up an image of the animal's surroundings. This organ is called the Jacobson's organ.

FACT FILE
Name Common lizard
Lacerta vivipara
Size 6 in long
Distribution Northern Asia, central and northern Europe

QUICK AS A FLASH

The common lizard chases prey among the sand dunes until it gets very close. Then at the last moment, it darts forward to seize the animal in its strong jaws.

Lizards have good eyesight, and they can see in color.

These long, strong toes grip surfaces well. Lizards are good at climbing.

Close up, you can see a small ear opening on the side of the head.

The long, thin body slides easily through grass and under stones.

A LUCKY BREAK

If an enemy grabs the lizard's tail, it has a very useful trick for escaping. It simply breaks off part of its tail and runs away. There are special weak points in the tail, so it does not hurt if it breaks off. A new tail gradually grows, although it does not have weak points like the old one.

Most of the bones in the tail can easily break apart, allowing the lizard to escape from a predator's grip.

The tail is often longer than the body. The lizard uses it for swimming, and to help balance its body when it is running or climbing.

GLOSSARY

Abdomen (invertebrates) *the rear part of the body*
Air bladder *a tiny air bubble found on the leaves of seaweed, causing them to float*
Algae *a simple plant, such as seaweed*
Alginic acid *a sticky substance produced by seaweed*
Amphibian *an animal, such as a frog, that can live both on land and in water*
Anemone *a simple sea creature that looks like a plant*
Antennae *a pair of feelers*
Antennules *a small pair of feelers*
Anus *an opening, usually at the rear of an animal's body, that releases waste material*
Apex *the pointed tip of a shell, for example*

Bacteria *microscopic organisms*
Barbel *a pointed feeler that sticks out from the jaw of certain fish and helps them to feel their way around*
Barnacle *a small, shelled, sea-dwelling animal that attaches itself to rocks and other objects*
Bivalve *a mollusk, such as a scallop, that has a two-part, hinged shell*
Bract *a leaflike structure that protects a flower*

Capsule (plants) *a kind of seed pod*
Carapace *the top part of the exoskeleton*
Carnivorous *meat eating*
Caudal fin *the tail fin, which helps a fish to steer and propel itself*
Chlorophyll *a green pigment in plants needed for photosynthesis*

Cilia *short, hairlike threads*
Cirri *slender tentacles*
Colony *a group of animals or plants of the same kind that live together*
Conch *a kind of seashell*
Continental shelf *a seabed that surrounds a continent that can be up to 219 yards deep*
Courtship *the behavior of animals prior to mating*

Detritus *fragments of dead material*
Dorsal fin *the back fin, which helps a fish to stay upright*

Echinodermata *sea animals with tube feet and a test*
Environment *the surroundings in which plants and animals live*
Estuary *the area where a river mouth flows into a sea*
Exoskeleton *a tough outer body covering*

Fertile *able to produce young*
Fin *an organ used for steering, balancing, and propelling*
Fungus *a group of living organisms that feeds on living or dead plants and animals*

Gills (fish) *the organs that fish use to take in oxygen from the water*
Gland *an organ that produces a chemical substance*
Gravitational pull *the sun and moon's force of gravity, which attracts the water of the oceans toward them causing tides*

Habitat *the natural home of an animal or plant*
Herbivore *a plant-eating animal*
Hermaphrodite *an animal that has both male and female parts*
Hibernate *to rest or sleep during cold months of the year*

Invertebrate *an animal that has no backbone*

Larva *a young, grublike stage of an animal that eventually develops into an adult*
Lateral line *a sensitive canal along each side of a fish's body*
Ligament (invertebrates) *an elasticlike substance that supports muscles*

Mantle *the part of a mollusk's skin that makes the shell*
Membrane *a thin, elastic skin*
Microscopic *anything too small to see without a microscope*
Mollusk *a soft-bodied animal, such as a snail or slug, that often has a shell*
Molt *to shed the skin or exoskeleton*
Mucus *a slimy, often poisonous substance*

Nare *a nostril*
Neap tide *the low tide*
Nutrient *a substance such as a mineral, which plants and animals need in order to stay healthy*

Omnivore *plant- and meat-eating animal*
Operculum *a protective cover, such as a fish's gill cover*
Organism *any living plant, animal, or fungus*

Palp *a feeler*
Parapodia *simple legs*
Parasite *an organism that lives in or on a living thing*
Parotid *a gland, sometimes poisonous, in front of the ears of certain animals*
Pectoral fin *a fin on the side of a fish that is used for balancing, turning, and stopping*
Pelvic fin *a fin that is used to help a fish stay upright*

Photosynthesis *the use of light by plants to produce energy for growing*
Phytoplankton *microscopic plants, such as algae*
Pigment *a substance that produces color in organisms*
Pincer *the front claw of some crustaceans, used for feeding, cleaning, and defense*
Plankton *tiny, floating sea creatures and plants*
Polyps *the tiny individual animals whose skeletons ma[ke] up a coral reef*
Predator *a meat-eating hunter*
Prey *any animal that is hunted and killed for food by another animal*
Proboscis *the long strawlike mouthpart of an animal, such as a whelk*
Pseudofeces *false droppings*

Radula *a filelike tongue*
Regeneration *the regrowth of part of the body by a pla[nt] or an animal*
Reproduce *to create offspring*
Rostrum *the beaklike formation on the head of certain kinds of animals, usually for protection*

Scale *a tough, platelike protective covering*
Scrape *a shallow hole that some birds make to lay eggs*
Sepal *the outer part of a flower that protects the bud*
Setae *special hairs on the body*
Shoal *a group of fish that swim together*
Silt *fine pieces of sand*
Siphon *a tube that allows water full of oxygen and foo[d] to pass into the body of an animal, such as a clam*
Spawn *to lay a mass of eggs*
Species *a group of similar organisms that can breed*
Sponge *a simple marine animal*
Spring tide *the high tide that occurs when the moon is full or new*
Stipe *a stalklike structure in plants and animals*
Streamlined *a shape that moves easily through air, water, or soil*
Sucker *an organ of an animal that clings to a surface suction*
Swimmeret *the paddlelike back leg of a crustacean*

Tentacle *a flexible feeler for touching, feeding, or smelling*
Territory *an area that an animal occupies and defen[ds] as its own*
Test *the outer layer of an animal, such as a sea urchin*
Thorax (invertebrates) *the middle part of the body containing the heart and lungs*
Transparent *see-through*

Ventral fin *the abdominal fin, which helps a fish to sta[y] upright*

Zoea *the larvae of crustaceans, such as crabs*
Zooplankton *microscopic animals, such as larvae*

INDEX

domen 22, 31, 62, 63, 76
bladder 41, 76
atross 10
gae 16-17, 24-25, 40-41, 76
ginic acid 40, 76
phibians 35, 66, 76
al fin 14
al vent 51
gelfish 8, 20-21
glerfish 11
tennae 23, 30, 59, 63, 76
tennules 55, 63, 76
us 28, 43, 49, 76
ex 47, 76
stotle's lantern 48

cteria 15, 76
rbels 61, 76
rnacles 36, 46, 47, 76
ls 44, 45
alves 36, 46, 76
act 64, 76
eding season 20, 45, 46
ttle star 50-51
wn seaweed 10, 40-41
ll rout 52
rrows 34, crab 68-69, lizard
    74, ragworm 58-59, toad 66

psule 46, 76
rapace 31, 54, 62, 76
rbon dioxide 40
nivores 10, 11, 13, 46, 56
dal fin 20, 52, 60, 76
elipeds 30
lorophyll 40-41, 76
a 71, 76
ri 58, 76
ms 10, 16-17
wn fish 10, 26-27
lonies 13, 36, 76
mpound eyes 31
nch 22, 76
nservation 9
ntinental shelf 9, 11, 76
ral reefs 8, 11, 13-14
urtship 12, 76
bs 34, edible 11, 54-55, fiddler 68-69,
    hermit 22-23, 34, piecrust 54-55, shore
    34, velvet 9, 54, 62-63
ustaceans 34, 35, 54

Diatoms 11
dorsal fin 14, 32, 38, 53, 60, 72, 76

Ear 67, 75
Echinodermata 48, 50, 76
environment 10, 76
estuaries 35, 76
exoskeleton 22-23, 30-31, 54, 76

Feathers 45
fertile 46, 76
fertilization 13, 20, 48, 50, 58
flock 44
flowers 64-65
food chains 11
fungus 15, 76

Gills 10, 76, fish 14, 40-41, gurnard 33,
    mudskipper 72-73, peacock worm 70-
        71, ragworm 58,
        rockling 61, scallop 36,
        sea lemon 42-43
    glands 65, 76
    grape coral 11, 13
    gravitational pull 9, 76
    green seaweed 10, 40
    gulls 10, 11
    gurnard 32-33

Habitat 8, 11, 12, 76
herbivores 10, 11, 76
hermaphrodites 42, 76
hibernation 35, 65, 74, 76
holdfast 40

Jacobson's organ 75
jellyfish 13, 56
jet propulsion 18

Kelp 11, 40, 34

Lateral line 14, 33, 73, 76
lichen 34
ligament 36, 76
limestone 8
limpet 11, 40, 34, 46
lizard 35, 74-75
lugworm 11
lungs 66

Mammals 10
mandarin fish 14-15
mangrove tree 72
mantle 16-17, 43, 76
marram grass 34
mating 20, 24, 42, 46, 66
membrane 33, 61, 74, 76
migration 35, 66
mollusks 10, 34, 35, 40, 44, 76, clam 16,
    octopus 18, sea lemon 42, whelk 46
molt 22, 54, 66, 76
mucus 76, fish 14-15, 26, peacock worm
    70, sea cucumber 28, sea lemon 43,
    sea slug 24, seaweed 41
mudskipper 72-73

mullet 10
mussels 11, 34, 46, 47

Nares 52, 61, 73, 76
natterjack toad 35, 66-67
neap tides 9, 76
nutrients 9, 76

Octopus 8, 18-19
omnivores 48, 59, 76
operculum 41, 47, 53, 61, 76
oxygen 14, 35, 39, 40, 58, 73
oystercatcher 35, 44-45
oysters 44

Palps 59, 76
paralyze 26, 56
parapodia 58-59, 76
parasites 40, 76
parotid glands 67, 76
peacock worm 70-71
pectoral fin 15, 20, 32-33, 53, 61, 72-73, 76
pelvic fin 15, 52, 60-61, 73, 76
periwinkle 9, 34
petals 64
photosynthesis 25, 30-31, 76
phytoplankton 11, 76
pied 45
pigments 19, 40-41, 76
pincers 76, crab 23, 54, 62-63, 68-69, sea
    urchin 49, starfish 50-51
plankton 11, 16, 22, 76
plants 9, 10, 11, 40-41, 34, 64-65
pollen sac 64-65
polyps 8, 13, 76
porpoises 10
prawns 11, 34, 60
proboscis 46-47, 76
pseudofeces 69, 76
pupil 19

Radula 18, 24, 42, 46, 76
ragworm 58-59
rays 14, 32-33, 40, 72-73
red seaweed 11, 40
regeneration 50, 76
reptiles 35, 74, 75
respiration 35
rockling 60-61
roots 64-65
rostrum 31, 76

Sand dunes 34, 35, 75
scales 21, 41, 61, 74, 76
scallops 34, 36-37
schools 21, 32, 60
scrape 44, 76
sea anemone 8, 10, 13, 26, 34, 56-57
sea cucumber 10, 28-29
sea horse 8, 12
sea lemon 9, 42-43
sea peas 64
sea pink 65
sea scorpion 10, 52-53
sea slug 24-25, 41, 42-43

sea snail 22, 40,
    46
sea urchin 11, 28,
    48-49
seaweeds 9, 11, 40-41
sense organs 14, 59
sepals 64, 76
setae 22, 31, 54-55, 76
shanny 11, 60-61
shrimp 30-31
silt 76
siphon 16-17, 76
skeleton 12, 13, 48, 50
spawn 76
spines 14, 29, 32, 38-39, 48-49, 50-51,
    52-53
splash zone 34
sponge 20, 24, 40, 42, 46, 76
spring tides 9, 34, 76
starfish 28, 36, 37, 48, 50-51
statocyst 30
sting-fish 52
stinging cells 13, 26, 57
stipe 40, 76
streamlined 10, 36, 76
suckers 18, 29, 51, 56, 72-73, 76
swimmerets 30, 76

Tadpoles 66
tail fin 14, 20, 32
tentacles 76, coral 13, ragworm 59, scallop
    37, sea anemone 10, 26, 56, 57, sea
    cucumber 28, 29, sea lemon 42,
    slug 25
territories 20, 44-45, 68, 76
test 48, 76
thorax 31, 76
thrift 35, 64
tides 9, 34-35, 40, 50, 57, 68, 70
topshell 34
tube feet 28-29, 48-49, 50-51
turtles 9, 35

Valves 34, 46
ventral fin 76

Weever fish 8, 40-41
whelk 22, 34, 42, 46-47
wrack 11, 34, 40-41

Zoea 63, 76
zooplankton 11, 76